THE KINGDOM

SIKA DEER, ASSATEAGUE NATIONAL WILDLIFE REFUGE, VIRGINIA, MAY 1989

THE KINGDOM

Wildlife in North America

Photographs by Art Wolfe   Text by Douglas Chadwick

A YOLLA BOLLY PRESS BOOK PUBLISHED BY

Sierra Club Books / San Francisco

IN ASSOCIATION WITH THE

National Wildlife Federation / Washington, D.C.

A YOLLA BOLLY PRESS BOOK

The Kingdom: Wildlife in North America was produced in association with the publisher at The Yolla Bolly Press, Covelo, California, under the supervision of James and Carolyn Robertson. Editorial and design staff: Diana Fairbanks, Nancy Campbell. Composition by Wilsted & Taylor, Oakland, California.

The Sierra Club, founded in 1892 by John Muir, has devoted itself to the study and protection of the earth's scenic and ecological resources—mountains, wetlands, woodlands, wild shores and rivers, deserts and plains. The publishing program of the Sierra Club offers books to the public as a nonprofit educational service in the hope that they may enlarge the public's understanding of the Club's basic concerns. The point of view expressed in each book, however, does not necessarily represent that of the Club. The Sierra Club has some sixty chapters coast to coast, in Canada, Hawaii, and Alaska. For information about how you may participate in its programs to preserve wilderness and the quality of life, please address inquiries to Sierra Club, 730 Polk Street, San Francisco, CA 94109.

Portions of this text appeared in the following periodicals: *Defenders of Wildlife* and *National Geographic*.

LIBRARY OF CONGRESS CATALOGING-IN-PUBLICATION DATA

Wolfe, Art.
  The kingdom: wildlife in North America / photographs by Art Wolfe; text by Douglas Chadwick.
      p.   cm.
  ISBN 0-87156-617-6
  1. Zoology—North America.   I. Wolfe, Art.   II. Title.   III. Chadwick, Douglas H.
QL151.W65   1990
591.97—dc20   90-34271
                                                         CIP

Printed and bound by Dai Nippon Printing Company, Ltd., Tokyo, Japan

10 9 8 7 6 5 4 3 2 1

PUBLISHED JOINTLY BY SIERRA CLUB BOOKS, SAN FRANCISCO, AND THE
NATIONAL WILDLIFE FEDERATION, WASHINGTON, D.C.

FIRST PAGE
Snow geese, New Mexico, March 1982

LAST PAGE
Short-billed dowitchers and dunlins, Grays Harbor, Washington, April 1989

YOUNG RACOONS, OLYMPIC NATIONAL FOREST, WASHINGTON, MARCH 1989

Contents

MUSK-OXEN, NUNIVAK ISLAND,
ALASKA, APRIL 1985

TRUMPETER SWANS, WASHINGTON, JANUARY 1983

Photographer's Introduction

DOUG CHADWICK and I met in October 1986 while boarding a flight to Moscow. During the following weeks we traveled as a team for *National Geographic*, documenting remote wilderness regions of the Soviet Union. Sharing the frustrations that accompany travel anywhere, but especially in that region, we often relied upon one another for social and psychological support. As our experiences multiplied our friendship grew, and, with it, our mutual respect. While staying in a biologist's camp on the Volga Delta, we discussed the idea of collaborating on a book. We decided the subject should be North American wildlife. We agreed to avoid duplicating the usual attempts to catalog every species. Our intent, rather, was to combine a series of essays with images that were more involving than the usual studies, aspiring finally to challenge the reader to view wildlife in a very different light. Our collaboration became *The Kingdom*.

Despite the fact that I could have readily selected from fourteen years' worth of wildlife photographs, most of the images in this book were photographed during 1989. There were two reasons for this. First, since much of Doug's text addresses contemporary ideas, I wanted the images to be correspondingly timely: an elk standing amidst charred Yellowstone pines (page 133), a reticent spotted owl perched within the ever-decreasing old-growth forest (page 163). Secondly, by working intensively during a short span of time, I felt that I could achieve a more cohesive visual statement.

The Kingdom presents four distinct photographic perspectives. I first concentrated primarily on classic wildlife portraiture, going to great lengths to get as close to my subjects as possible. My ultimate goal was to freeze the instant of contact between photographer and animal. For instance in the portraits of the lynx (page 185), gray wolf (page 115), and Alaskan brown bear (page 157), environment and behavior are secondary to the mesmerizing moment of visual contact. By including this type of image I've attempted to share the spirit of the moment with our readers. Rather than allowing them to remain detached I want to affect their emotions, whether evoking a smile or something deeper. In the American bison portrait (page 22) I compromised my safety in order to get close enough to create a more abstract image. A winter's night spent in the mist of a geyser left this bison with frosted fur. As you look at this image the frost patterns first draw your attention; then the large, dark eyes come

The trumpeter swan (Cygnus buccinator) is the largest waterfowl on the globe. Six feet long from bill to tail tip, with wings eight feet across shining white in the sun, these birds in flight might be imagined to have the approximate dimensions of angels. In the 1930s it was feared that the last trumpeter had vanished. Its breeding habitat had been transformed by agriculture, its migrating flocks shot down for meat, feathers, and the soft porous skin, which was turned into tens of thousands of powder puffs. But a small nonmigratory population was uncovered, holding out high in the Rockies in the Yellowstone ecosystem. In the decades since then its numbers have slowly built up, and managers have transplanted small groups from this area to other refuges in the West and Midwest. What no one realized is that trumpeter swans by the hundreds or more remained all along in remote portions of Alaska and British Columbia. Biologists had assumed that they were part of the North's large population of tundra swans (Cygnus columbianus), which closely resemble trumpeters. But until the trumpeters of the Lower 48 become more widely distributed and can reestablish some of their former migratory patterns, they will remain one of the most vulnerable species south of Canada.

forth to present an unsettling challenge. On the lighter side the straightforward portraits of the porcupine (page 132) and the tufted puffin (page 52) are humorous. To this end habitat and behavior were somewhat neglected.

A second and decidedly more important perspective was key to the evolution of *The Kingdom*: capturing an animal in its natural environment. Douglas Chadwick's text speaks as much to habitat as to the animals themselves. Therefore, I began stepping back from my subjects, giving the images a larger sense of place. In the photographs of the black-tailed deer (page 166), black-legged kittiwake (page 183), and black bear (page 63), habitat is as important as the animal. I believe I've been most successful when animal and habitat fuse into an almost abstract pattern of shape and color, as in the photographs of the prairie falcon (page 75), the hoary marmot (page 17), and the moth (page 196).

The third photographic perspective takes an even greater abstract turn. I've long been an admirer of German artist M. C. Escher's beguiling use of negative and positive spaces. Capturing natural patterns on film has long been a favorite theme of mine. Pattern, simply the repetition of similar shapes, is clearly evident in the images of shorebirds (page 204), northern gannets (page 168), and snow geese (page 1). As in the portrait series, environment has almost no role in these images. Rather, it is the two-dimensional nature of the image that allows each element, or, in this case, animal, to be as important as the next, while the surrounding negative space warrants equal attention.

Lastly, a book on North American wildlife would clearly be remiss if it neglected behavior. Artistic action shots are difficult to achieve, and therefore they presented a worthy challenge to me while I traversed our designated territory in preparation for this book. The results include a snow-spattered coyote (page 18) standing over a starved elk in forage-depleted Yellowstone National Park; mountain goat kids (page 148) playing tirelessly like rambunctious children on the summer snowfields of Glacier National Park; a fifty-ton humpback whale breaching in the icy waters of southeast Alaska (page 51); and Alaskan brown bears fighting energetically in the Brooks River (page 41).

As you proceed through the pages that follow, it is our hope that you will come away with a slightly altered perspective on the wildlife that share our continent, and an increased awareness of the need to preserve their natural habitat.

ART WOLFE
SEATTLE, WASHINGTON
DECEMBER 1989

List of Photographs

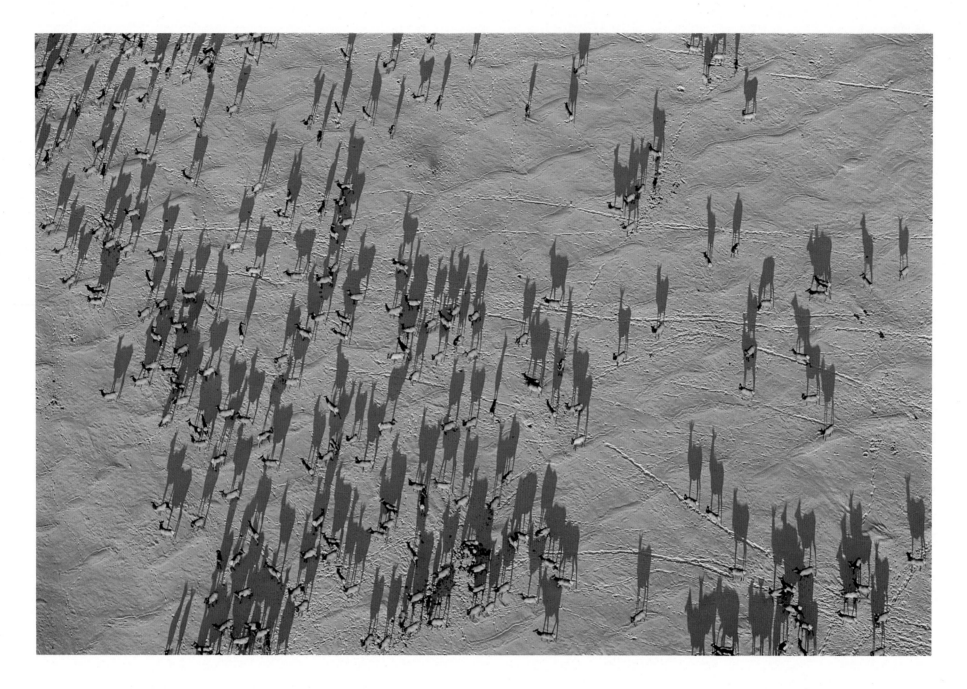

ELK HERD, NATIONAL ELK REFUGE, WYOMING, FEBRUARY 1990

BLACK-TAILED DEER, OLYMPIC NATIONAL PARK, WASHINGTON, AUGUST 1984

HOARY MARMOT, CANADIAN ROCKIES,
ALBERTA, JULY 1989

COYOTE WITH ELK CARCASS, YELLOWSTONE NATIONAL PARK, WYOMING, FEBRUARY 1989

CHAPTER ONE

The Front

T HERE ARE POOLS OF DREAMS, and there are pools of genes. We draw creativity and meaning from both. I'd rather hike in wild country among free-ranging animals than do almost anything else. I know a place where wildlife communities are arrayed in a tumult of Rocky Mountain scenery that strikes fresh hope loose with each step, and I hike there as often as I can. To me it represents a special entryway to the kingdom. By the kingdom I mean all of North America's native species—and all of our human feelings, ideas, and imaginings about the creatures that share this continent. No real border has ever existed between the nature of the kingdom around us and the nature of the kingdom within. To explore one is to explore the other. This is what leads me to make trip after trip through good, strong country animated by wild lives, such as the stretch of the Rockies that I have in mind. It is a journey of discovery that has no boundaries and no end.

In northern Montana the Continental Divide is built from layers of limestone, shale, and a silica-bound clay known as argillite. It is all basically sea-bottom muck, transmuted into banded stone and thrust into the blue depths of the sky—a reef in the atmosphere with clouds foaming across its surface. The prevailing winds come from the west, losing heat and moisture as they wash up against the forested western slopes. Then, grown cool and heavy, the air mass tumbles down the Divide's sharp eastern edge, cascading over cliffs and through glacier-sculpted basins and river-cut canyons, singing, shaping the branches of subalpine fir and limber pine, spilling onto the shortgrass foothills that mark the beginning of the Great Plains. The invisible currents regularly reach gale force. Every so often hurricane-force gusts fling gravel the size of marbles around and flip some more trailer houses off their moorings out on the Blackfeet Indian reservation.

This abrupt, powerful conjunction of the peaks and the prairie is known as the Rocky Mountain Front. I love to walk in the big winds loosed there, with orchestrations of hawks and eagles on all sides. Several times when conditions were just right during the frozen months, I've hiked to the upper end of a Front lake, strapped on ice skates, held open a tarpaulin—or just my windbreaker—and flown down to the lower end.

Elk and mule deer winter by the thousands in the foothills. On the escarpments and talus slopes above dwell bighorn sheep, wintering where air blasts keep the

A coyote (Canis latrans) stands over an elk carcass in Yellowstone National Park. During 1988 a severe drought was followed by spectacular fires, which caused food shortages for some of the hoofed animals. A higher number than usual, including this elk, succumbed to the effects of starvation over winter. The coyotes dined well. Coyotes are good hunters as well as expert scavengers. But at twenty to fifty pounds they are too small to successfully prey upon elk. The member of the canine family that could help keep elk populations in balance with the available food supply is the gray wolf (Canis lupus). A growing number of biologists favor reintroducing this native species to North America's—and the world's— first national park. Wolves and wildfire: the two natural forces managers fought so hard to control in the past are perhaps the very factors that would most improve the health and habitat of Yellowstone's hoofed animals over the long run.

19

ground largely free of deep snow. Mountain goats use still higher, steeper outcroppings, being more specialized than sheep both for climbing and for pawing through snow to get at food. Sometimes when everything is buried by a heavy storm or icy crusts, I'll find goats standing face to face with the bare, vertical rock between the ledges. They seem to be eating the stone in desperation. In fact, they are licking and scraping off its coat of lichen.

Grizzlies, hereabouts, go by the familiar name "grizz," and they generally hibernate in dens high on the mountainsides. They want some measure of privacy and a thick snowpack for insulation while they snooze. One of the first things grizz do after emerging in the spring is patrol beneath the sheep and goat cliffs for hoofed bodies brought down by climbing accidents or, more often, avalanches. Most of the bears then swing on downslope into the foothills for a while, and a few venture out onto the open prairie. They are mainly stalking the new, tender plant tissues that first appear at lower elevations: grass and sedge shoots, wild celery stalks and tubers, lily bulbs, and so on. But thawing carcasses of winter-killed elk and deer are part of the foothills food supply during green-up time.

There used to be bison carcasses as well. The region may have had both typical plains bison, *Bison bison americanus*, and a smaller, shaggier, darker variety described by early travelers in the Rockies and uplands to the west. They called it the mountain buffalo. No one knows whether this was a race of plains bison or of the lesser known, slightly heavier woodland bison, *Bison bison athabascae*, once widespread in the continent's northern, or boreal, forests. Not so very long ago bison also roamed eastern deciduous forests from Georgia to New York: in 1612 a Sir Samuel Argoll was potting buffalo with his musket along the Potomac, where a suburb of Washington, D.C., now sprawls. No one is sure what kind those were either.

In any given year prior to the arrival of Europeans an estimated 35 to 100 million bison were living in North America. That is a biomass comparable to the combined weight of every man, woman, and child alive in the United States, Canada, and Mexico at the moment, and it probably represented the single greatest accumulation of a large mammal species the earth had yet produced anywhere. By 1894 North America contained 20 plains bison in the wild, several hundred on private ranches and in zoos, and perhaps 250 woodland bison in Canada. The other 99.99 percent had been liquidated, half of them in just the half-century between 1830 and 1880, when the buffalo hunters rolled west from the Mississippi like dry lightning, pouring water on rifle barrels overheated by nonstop firing and bragging that they pissed on the things to cool them down when their canteens ran dry. For years after the smoke and carcass stink drifted away a plainsman could make a living gathering bones and carting them to the railways to be shipped east and ground for potash.

A few score woodland bison can still be found wild in northern Alberta's Wood Buffalo National Park. A handful have been transplanted to Nahanni National Park in the Northwest Territories. Not one eastern bison, whatever they were, survives. Nor a single mountain bison, whatever genes and potential they may have carried.

BISON, YELLOWSTONE NATIONAL PARK, WYOMING, FEBRUARY 1989

BISON, YELLOWSTONE NATIONAL PARK,
WYOMING, FEBRUARY 1989

Nor are any free-ranging plains bison left near the Rocky Mountain Front. Cattle partially fill the emptied niche, as ranchers tend to haul winter-killed livestock out to "bone piles" and leave them there for scavengers rather than try to bury the big carcasses in hard-frozen soil. Eagles and ravens still have the remains of a big bovid to pack off into the sky, while coyotes drag away the grizzlies' leftovers to gnaw on in the brush.

Any spring meat a grizzly happens upon may provide a crucial nutrition boost. The bears come out of hibernation depleted of energy reserves, and usually continue losing weight all spring. They barely keep even on early summer forage. Not until the plants begin putting forth seeds—their precious offspring, swaddled in oils and sugars—can the bears really begin putting on fat for the winter to come. In the Rockies the main cause of plump grizz are huckleberries. Next in importance are whitebark pine nuts, which the bears raid from squirrel caches in the ground along the high ridges where these pines grow.

Some alpinists climbing Mount Cleveland—Glacier National Park's tallest peak, and a respectable climbing challenge—struggled up the final pitches handhold by handhold, and hauled themselves onto the summit. They put down their ropes and carabiners, looked around to see the view, were greeted by a couple of roly-poly grizzly bears, and climbed right back down again. I've encountered bears on the crowns of peaks nearly as steep. A number of them make special treks each summer to mountaintops where certain insects gather: cutworm moths on some summits, ladybug beetles on others, grasshoppers on still others. These are even more concentrated energy packets than fruits and nuts, and the bears roam like minor landslides across the high slopes, turning over rocks to lick up the insects seething underneath.

Silver-tipped bears ripening in berry patches, elk, long-bearded, winter-colored goats, a weathered bison skull staring up from a marsh, a prairie falcon hurtling at gale force toward a sharp-tailed grouse. And what else did I find along the Front? Cougar tooth marks in the neck of a dead mule deer. Lynx. Wolverine fur. . . .

I tick the animal list off to friends without further comment, and they say, ah, you had a good trip. They know that the reward was not in the tally of wild things seen but in the thoughts and feelings engendered by their presence. How many? How rare? How close? How bright? Similarly, the challenge of conservation involves much more than saving or losing individual species. It concerns the range of experiences, images, ideas, and emotions that will be available to us in the future from contact with wild beings and wild surrounds. Conservation is therefore about the dimensions of humanity—the promise of the kingdom within. The question is also whether or not we can conserve the overriding resource compounded of the animals' welfare and ours—wholeness. A sense of belonging and continuity. Common ground. Community. Or maybe communion. The words dance close but never seem to alight. The best I can do is continue with the list of what I saw. Red fox. Black bear. Mountain bluebird. Ah. Good trip.

And long-billed curlews in a hayfield. A Blackfeet family cutting firewood. Mir-

The shoulder hump that characterizes the bison (Bison bison) consists of muscles attached to projections from the backbone. These extra muscles are needed to power the beast's massive head. The male's prominent beard adds to the overall impression of size during dominance displays, while the thick, matted hair of the head in both sexes helps absorb the impact of blows during battles between herd members. By using its broad forehead as a shovel, the bison is able to reach grasses and other winter forage buried beneath deep and drifted snow. Stockmen have attempted to blend the hardiness and self-sufficiency of the bison with the meat qualities of the cow in a hybrid known as the beefalo. In theory, beefalo would be able to use the open ranges of the West through winter without the constant care and feeding required by cattle, thereby cutting down ranchers' costs considerably. In practice, however, it has proved difficult to maintain a true-breeding beefalo line.

rors, ribbons, a few feathers, and tobacco offerings scattered through a holy site at the base of a peak. Shooting stars. Lightning. Rainbows. A rancher who said his brother heard an unmistakable howl last autumn. Didn't care for it one bit; music to eat cows by, he figured. But there it was: Wolf. Beaver. Badger. Goldeneye duck. . . .

The heft and breadth of life's inventory here result from the Front's excellent connections. On one side it blends into agricultural land with a very sparse human population. On the other it merges with an intact mountain ecosystem that includes the Bob Marshall Wilderness, Great Bear Wilderness, Scapegoat Wilderness, and Glacier National Park. This northern Continental Divide ecosystem and the gene pools that it harbors connect in turn to wildlands along the Divide extending far north into British Columbia and Alberta, where the wolverines that reappeared in Montana several decades ago came from, and where the wolves returning right now started out.

Compared to the hubbub of modern industrial society, the Front is mighty slow paced. The ranchlands don't change much from one decade to the next, and through many stretches of the backcountry, you would be hard pressed to tell which century you were in. But timeless is not a fitting description of this weld of mountains and plains. The place is steeped in time. Its current inventory of life snuffles and soars within a stone framework of life's course through the eons.

One reason I envision the Front's mountain wall as a reef in the air is that it has embedded within it a thick band of marine structures termed stromatolites. They represent mats and mounds of microbes that formed in shallow Precambrian seas nearly two billion years ago. These cyanobacteria—previously described as blue-green algae—may have been the first organisms to form tangible communities beyond mere swarms of single cells. And they changed the game for virtually all organisms thereafter, for cyanobacteria invented the type of photosynthesis whereby carbon dioxide is taken in and oxygen is given off. At the time the envelope of gases around the planet was dominated by carbon dioxide. Oxygen was present only in trace amounts. Before long, green cells had pumped the atmosphere full of oxygen.

The stromatolite layer lies in overthrust strata near the crest of the Divide, up where the first colors of dawn collect. Perched on one of those ledges in a deluge of wind, I inhaled and thought over its contents. The very air of our planet is a by-product of its creatures—the result of natural genetic engineering. This was a startling idea when first deduced. Unfortunately, smog, acid rain, and depletion of the ozone layer have made the link between the atmosphere and the activities of organisms considerably easier to understand. The green cells' work is being reversed. Carbon dioxide is building up rapidly through the burning of fossil fuels combined with the clearing and burning of tropical rainforests. As most people are now aware, this has led to a measurable warming trend coupled with a modest rise in sea levels: the start of the greenhouse effect.

Managers of public lands such as Glacier National Park and the adjoining National Forest are used to planning for the impact of visitors, roads, commercial developments, and the like, trying to stay ahead of projected increases. Suddenly, their pro-

MOUNTAIN GOATS, GLACIER NATIONAL PARK, MONTANA, JULY 1989

Snow drifts past the remains of a musk-ox (Ovibos moschatus). One certainty about life is that it comes to an end. Another is that as surely as winter leads into spring, each life form endlessly renews itself—unless it is beset by new pressures in the environment. Seamen hunting bowhead and other whales off arctic shores often wintered over in Eskimo territory. They gunned down herd after herd of musk-oxen to stock their larders with fresh meat, taking advantage of the animals' tendency to form a defensive circle rather than flee. As firearms spread through the North, musk-oxen were quickly reduced from a circumpolar species to a few isolated herds in Canada. In 1929 a number were shipped from a remnant group in Greenland to Nunivak Island off Alaska's west coast. The transplanted herd increased under full protection, and has since been used to restock portions of former habitat along Alaska's North Slope, where musk-oxen had not been seen since the 1850s.

jections are also supposed to take into account a possible further rise in the average daily temperature of as much as six to ten degrees Fahrenheit over the next century. Plus accompanying changes in global weather patterns. When U.S. Forest Service specialists calculate future timber reserves, for instance, they have to ask themselves whether certain types of conifers will even regrow in traditional habitats after cutting a few decades from now. What about the animals that depend upon those trees? No one has ever had to draw up plans for a new climatic epoch before. What will become of species already rare or endangered? What will be the shape of the North American kingdom when my children's children begin taking hikes of their own?

The Front may not have the answers, but it offers all kinds of perspectives. Toward the base of its cliffs are limestone caves floored with the dung of giant ground sloths. Fossils of mammoths, woolly rhinoceros, and huge ancestral bison wait nearby in the foothills. Whenever heavy runoff from rains or melting snow cuts the gullies deeper, more ruins of Ice Age megafauna spill out into the light. Their time on earth came to a close during the last major warming trend, which marked the end of the Pleistocene some ten thousand years back.

Montana paleontologist John Horner once stopped by the funky little rock shop in the mostly ghost town of Bynum along the Front. He picked up a cardboard box of fossil bones. They were unidentified and, being quite small, had been priced a lot cheaper than the mammoth and rhino parts stacked on other tables. Horner fiddled with the dusty bargain bones in the box and laid them out in his mind. What he came up with were tiny dinosaurs. Babies, as a matter of fact.

Infant dinosaurs had been found in only one place on the globe before. Horner traced the Bynum fossils to the dryland pastures of a nearby cattle ranch. Within a few years he had unearthed enough dinosaur nesting sites and stone carcasses to help overhaul our entire conception of the giant reptiles. His evidence revealed them to be migratory over long distances, highly sociable, strongly maternal, and, judging from the growth rates of youngsters that stayed at their mothers' sides, very likely warm-blooded.

I remember slowly chipping a hadrosaur, or duck-billed dinosaur, femur free from the shale while Horner described the grizzlies that had been wandering near his field camp that spring. I remember, too, a lizard—a horned toad—making its way through the prairie weeds where I was picking up hadrosaur eggshells. It made me wonder anew why the most advanced reptile line—the dinosaurs—should have been the one to meet with oblivion.

A couple of miles away was another type of excavation, enclosed by a strong wire mesh. A number of such small fenced sites are spaced along the Front. They are scarcely noticeable in the sweep of the grasslands. Inside the earth at each one is a nuclear missile silo.

To have atomic warheads planted so near a preeminent dinosaur research project makes a kind of cosmic sense, I guess. Although God alone knows the details of why the dinosaurs' 140-million-year-long reign ended in a global wave of extinction,

MUSK-OX SKULL, NUNIVAK ISLAND, ALASKA, APRIL 1985

ELK, YELLOWSTONE NATIONAL PARK, WYOMING, JANUARY 1989

more and more hard data point toward a cataclysm. And the leading cataclysmic theory involves a comet or meteor striking the planet and causing the equivalent of a nuclear holocaust, with fire storms and clouds of dust and soot choking off the sunlight.

So your imagination hikes back and forth among the windy revelations of the Front, up and down the depositions of time. If life begins to strike you as a less orderly procession than before, it also seems possessed of tremendous resiliency. That it will carry on in some form, come what may, seems probable. Yet the particular forms that have emerged through the tumult of ages to animate the present hours become, to me, all the more miraculous. All the more precious. Snowshoe hare. Rainbow trout. Moose. Migrating swan. Good trip.

During a visit to Siberia not long ago my thoughts returned to the Front. While U.S. observers stood by, Soviet military personnel incinerated their own nuclear missiles. It may have been one of the critical events in the long-playing drama of the biosphere. Or it may prove to have been hollow symbolism. Time will tell without fail.

I wasn't one of the official observers. I just happened to be passing through, observing Evenk reindeer herders and Yakuts carving mammoth ivory gathered from the permafrost. That part of the world has played a key role in the history of North American wildlife communities. The majority of our continent's existing large mammals arose in Eurasia and reached the New World through what is now Siberia and the Soviet Far East.

The Miocene epoch, lasting from 27 million years ago until about 7 million years ago, saw the appearance of most modern mammal families. Around the middle of that period the climate started to cool. Glaciers grew in the high latitudes. As more and more surface water turned solid, becoming locked up as ice and snow, sea levels dropped. A land bridge emerged between Asia and North America. The two continents remained in contact, exchanging fauna until well into the next epoch, the Pliocene, when the climate warmed. Roughly 3 million years ago, in the late Pliocene, things began to cool off again, and the Old and New Worlds were once more linked.

Then came the true Ice Age of land-scraping glaciers a mile or two thick and as wide as the continent—the Pleistocene, now thought to have commenced 1.7 million years back. Throughout much of this period the route across the northern Pacific was not nearly as narrow as its usual name, the Bering Land Bridge, might suggest. Paleontologists speak instead of Beringia, a land mass extending from the Kolyma River in the modern-day U.S.S.R. to Canada's Mackenzie River in the Yukon. At different times during the Pleistocene, Beringia was grassy steppe, then the northern forest called taiga, and finally tundra. A good portion of it remained unglaciated, as did much of Siberia. Beringia thus not only joined the continents but was a major Ice Age refugium and evolutionary center in its own right.

One by one they traveled the trans-Pacific span, most of them in more or less the same form as their current descendants: Bison. Musk-oxen. Mountain sheep. Moun-

Throughout the northern latitudes the long winter months are the crucible of natural selection, claiming the weaker animals and leaving the better adapted individuals. Among elk (Cervus elaphus) the sex ratio is approximately equal at birth, but populations on the whole contain significantly fewer males than females. Males suffer higher death rates for several reasons. First, they are more exploratory than females. Inexperienced yearling males are particularly prone to run into trouble as they disperse from their mother's home range, whereas yearling females stick closer to home. Secondly, bulls sometimes wound or kill one another while battling during the autumn breeding season. Thirdly, even if they escape outright damage from rivals, the bulls expend a tremendous amount of energy bugling, fighting, guarding their harem of females, and courting them throughout the rut, and they enter the winter with seriously depleted fat reserves. This pattern of increased mortality among males is fairly typical for the deer family as a whole. For that matter, it describes the situation for a great many polygamous mammals. The ability of a single male to breed several females makes males more "expendable." It also encourages sexual dimorphism. That is, when a male can ensure more descendants by winning a large number of mates than by sharing care of the young with a single mate, evolution puts a premium on males that are larger and more aggressive than the opposite sex.

29

MULE DEER, POINT LOBOS, CALIFORNIA, SEPTEMBER 1989

tain goat. Elk. Deer. Caribou. Moose. Great brown bear. Polar bear: it developed from the brown bear perhaps one hundred thousand years ago, and the two species are still genetically similar enough that they have interbred and produced fertile offspring in a zoo. Skunk. Mink. Lemming. Even freshwater pike colonized North America from Eurasia, swimming across Beringia's streams. Good trip. Wolf. Coyote. Lynx. . . .

Not that our continent didn't have its own lines of dogs and cats, all the way up to dire wolves and saber-toothed cats, which may have specialized in hunting mastodons. For native hoofed fauna there were camels, rhinos, horses, and the pronghorn antelope. On the whole, however, the immigrants represented newer types with more complex social behavior and communication abilities. This presumably gave them an advantage, especially in fast-changing environments, as they competed with the original inhabitants and either displaced them or carved out new niches in between.

But competition alone doesn't explain why such a large proportion of North America's wonderfully rich mixture of Pleistocene creatures came to an end as the epoch did. As much as 70 percent of the existing species vanished, most of them between fifteen to nine thousand years ago, with the peak of extinction coming about eleven thousand years ago.

Well, the climate changed. The ice let loose its grip, gave up the siege, slunk back to brood over the poles; the modern epoch, the Holocene, finally came into leaf, and the old guard couldn't cope with the new, hotter environments. So runs the traditional explanation. Yet the climatic change appears to have been less sudden than the collapse of the animal populations. While the Pleistocene was officially over ten thousand years ago, the relatively warm weather we know didn't really get underway until some seven thousand years ago. Besides, the Ice Age included any number of earlier warm spells, or interglacials. Many came on at the same pace as the Holocene, if not faster, and reached the same temperatures, if not hotter ones. In truth, the Holocene is only another interglacial; it merely happened to be the first in which we had geologists around devising names. Ironically, the greenhouse effect may make a genuinely different epoch of it yet.

The question remains: Why did so many animals that survived earlier transitions to hotter weather fail to adjust to this last one? Their habitats didn't vanish altogether; they shifted northward with the vegetation zones as temperatures increased. At least some of the beasts that went out of business should have been more than able to shift along with them. They had before. As far as we can tell, good mammoth range still exists in the north country's tundra and taiga. For that matter, why should the New World have lost a notably larger percentage of fauna than the Old World did? The difference could lie with yet another species that arrived from Eurasia: *Homo sapiens.*

Paleo-Indians peopled Siberia perhaps thirty to forty thousand years ago, possibly earlier, and almost surely followed herds of mammoths, rhinos, and other hulking, woolly groceries along the major river valleys that flow northward from central Asia.

A mule deer (Odocoileus hemionus) makes its wary way through the low-lying branches of windswept conifer trees along the California coast. When alarmed, white-tailed deer—sometimes called flag-tails—raise their tails straight up. This conspicuous signal serves to alert other deer in the area that danger is near. Mule deer achieve the same group warning effect by bounding away in a series of high, attention-getting leaps called stotting, in which all four feet strike the ground at once.

31

Each fall as the last salmon run from the northern Pacific up Alaska's coastal streams to spawn, bald eagles (Haliaetus leucocephalus) gather along the Chilkat River to hook the big fish with their talons. Brown bears and the occasional wolf join in the feast. Gulls and ravens squabble over the leftovers. Toward the end of the spawning run as salmon begin to weaken, die, and wash onto the shores, there is more than enough to fill every belly. The Chilkat Valley hosts the continent's greatest congregation of bald eagles, three to four thousand strong at its peak—a remarkable figure, considering that the entire Lower 48 held no more than fifteen hundred breeding pairs at last count. The Chilkat Valley has also been the scene of a struggle between timber interests and conservationists, who fear that extensive clearcut logging would lead to siltation of streams and a decline in salmon numbers. North America's largest raptor after the condor is clearly marked by a snow-white head and tail in adults. Juveniles have mottled brown plumage that they retain until age four or even five, when they first begin breeding. They mate for life and return year after year to the same nest built from stout twigs piled several feet high on a treetop or cliff side.

Widespread hints exist that some hunting bands may have veered across to the New World at about the same time. However, the experts disagree on the true age of artifacts and geologic deposits at key sites. All things considered, the earliest colonists of which we can be certain were Paleo-Indians of the Diuktai culture, who crossed Beringia beginning about thirteen thousand years ago and dispersed fairly quickly toward warmer countrysides. Some forty-five hundred to five thousand years ago, a second, smaller pulse of emigration occurred as Paleo-Eskimos of the Summaginsk culture kayaked from the Chukchi Peninsula to Alaska and went on to claim the New World's arctic rim.

To pass southward from Beringia the Paleo-Indians must have followed the gap that opened about twelve thousand years ago between the main continental ice sheet, the Laurentide, and the sheet that covered the West from the Rockies to the coast, the Cordilleran. This glacier-free corridor led through Canada's Northwest Territories along the general course of the Nahanni River. The Slave Indians living there today know it as Nahadeh, Powerful River. It is a stone gray, uncoiling spirit with hot springs and limestone caverns dripping from its sides.

I have floated Powerful River a couple of times, and once skied part of its length in late winter, keeping to the ice near shore. Since the Nahanni was flowing strong before geologic forces began to twist and uplift this region, it slices directly through three towering ranges of the Mackenzie Mountains. Deep in those canyons between white, avalanching mountain walls and ice caves that entomb prehistoric sheep, I found it easy to envision instead glaciers grinding away on both sides, myself bound for a brandnew land downstream. When you have a fifty-pound pack on your back and twenty miles to cover before dark, it can't hurt to daydream a greater destiny for yourself. And, anyway, I did feel swept up within a larger pattern of movement.

The trail I was gliding on had been tramped out by more than fifty wolves—an unusually large crowd, resulting from the temporary union of several packs. Their paws overlaid the hoofprints of a herd of around two hundred caribou. All day the river thrummed beneath our mixed tracks. Sometimes it talked about where the ice was thin and current-eaten. Mostly it just told itself stories, passing them endlessly along from its headwaters. Then at night northern lights would appear in the river of stars above, and howl the sky full of green fire.

Once the Paleo-Indians passed through the Nahanni region many, if not most, are believed to have continued on a route that ran along the eastern edge of the icebound Rockies. In other words they traveled southward along the edge of the Front, which, in its larger sense, extends from around Calgary, Alberta, nearly to Helena, Montana. The wayfarers were no longer Diuktai. They had become Clovis people. Their name comes from the distinctive fluted spear points that appeared about twelve thousand years ago, and outline the expansion of this culture across the Americas over the next millennium.

The march of the Clovis people coincides with the peak of mammal extinctions. How much of the die-off should rightly be laid at these spear-bearers' feet is anyone's

BALD EAGLES IN COTTONWOOD TREES, ALASKA, NOVEMBER 1983

guess. And guesses abound. I've read scenarios in which the New World beasts, completely unfamiliar with humans, mill dazedly around while the invaders plunder them at will and herd them en masse off cliffs. The model for this is remote islands such as the Galapagos, whose species show little or no fear of people. But then they have little or no experience with mammalian predators of any kind. North America's fauna had plenty, and I doubt they were so naive. My own hunch is that Clovis hunters did exterminate some populations, but mainly those already made vulnerable by habitat changes that reduced their living space and interfered with breeding success. What is going on at the moment is not all that different. Except these days, *we* are the ones changing the habitat, as well as finishing off the creatures in trouble as a result.

Interesting how the growing length of the endangered species list has made us more willing to contemplate the role of prehistoric humans in mass extinctions. Until recently we were more inclined to picture "primitive" human bands grinding along at subsistence level, barely holding their own in a world of harsh elements and ferocious beasts. Yet ours is not a young, frail-but-ingenious species emerging among brutish forms from an earlier time, however much we may like to think of ourselves that way. *Homo sapiens* is as old as most of the mammals in North America, older than many, and as tough as they come. And humankind—*Homo one-thing-or-another*—has been around for millions of years. What is new under the sun is, first, our growing awareness that we do indeed have the capacity for overwhelming the communities of life around us. The second new thing is our conscious effort to save those communities.

While the overall influence of people upon animal communities throughout history is difficult to gauge, the influence of animal communities upon people is clearer. They made us. As predators and competitors, they put us together and kept us together. As prey, they were the foundation and strength of our culture, the material basis of our success. Overall, they were the source of many of our patterns of behavior and thought—our teachers. At one time virtually everyone alive was both part of the kingdom and an expert student of it.

At the most basic level, animals taught us foraging techniques and told us what was sprouting, what bulbs, buds, fruits, and nuts were ripe. They taught us about environmental conditions. Not as we think of environmental conditions now, in which wildlife is the proverbial canary in the mine shaft—or roseate spoonbill in the drying Everglades—warning us, by perishing, that the life support system is breaking down. I mean that they told us about the potential for doing *well* on the land. They showed us the patterns of growth, the routes to shelters, the best wintering grounds, the promise of rainfall.

You can see last winter's snow depth in the spring condition of an antelope's coat or in the number of twin fawns skittering behind does in early summer. You can see tomorrow's storm in the winnowing flight of a snipe. If this bird begins its song before early evening and circles lower than usual, a low-pressure front is moving in.

CARIBOU, ALASKA RANGE, ALASKA, AUGUST 1987

SNOWSHOE HARE, MONTANA, OCTOBER 1987

High pressure and the promise of clearing sometimes send the creature so far upward you can no longer make out its body; only the hollow, haunted notes. The music doesn't come from this shorebird's throat. It issues from two outer tailfeathers, strummed by the wind as the snipe dives.

In my mind I journey with a Clovis band along the Front, and I see each of the creatures there not as wild but as existing on exactly the same terms that I do. They just have different skills. I would not know what "tame" means. Throughout my time, and my grandparents' time, and through all the times since the first tales were told in my tribe, animals and people have exchanged bodies, spirits, and the things they know. They dream of each other. Maybe they dream each other into being. I am their brother, their slayer, their mourner, and the one who sings of their beauty. Their beauty is ours. Their abundance is ours. In these days before metal they are the riches we seek. They bring the good life. Fat times. Easy living. Status. And the wealth of knowledge. They are how I know the meaning of speed, strength, grace, virility, fecundity. And the way I measure the seasons. And the reason I stay alive and how I define what I do to live and the things I accomplish and how I name my children and the way I speak to the gods. What am I myself but an animal at prayer?

Now I am a Blackfeet Indian roaming along the Front in the buffalo times before the coming of the white men. The horse has been gone from the prairies since the Ice Age ended. Soon Spanish explorers will bring it back to the New World. We will call it the elk-dog, and be afraid when we first see it. Then we will become its masters and then masters of distance, looking over the plains from the backs of spotted ponies, racing like the wind off the peaks. But for now, we still drag travois behind dogs when we move camp.

Last night I had a dream, and into it walked my spirit guide. He came to tell me it was time to move again and build a new lodge. He is one of the coyote people, more clever than any of the bear people. More clever even than the raven people. At least that is how I have always felt. Maybe that is why coyote chose to become my guide. Whatever coyote himself dreams almost always comes true.

Coyote told me where to build the new lodge, and when, and how, so that it would please the sun. He told me in which direction to open its face, and the way to paint the markings for the winds, and how his own image would walk on the other side among the moon and stars. I forget how he spoke about these matters. Dream language is more than words. It is like a silver spider web leading from the sky to the ground that is woven each night and disappears with the dawn. It is like the chinook wind that comes suddenly in winter and melts the snow with its warm breath.

Maybe coyote knows my language. I am learning his. Since coyote became my guide I have tried to listen carefully so I can tell when a coyote man is calling to a coyote woman, and when the woman is calling to her children. I know the songs of challenge and the songs of coming together, the chants of mating in the cold moon of January, and the cries of the young and unsure. Anyone can learn to hear who listens with care. Anyone can sing who practices. I used to squeal like a rabbit to bring

Winter is a good time for observing the habits of the snowshoe hare (Lepus americanus). The distinctive tracks left in the snow by its exceptionally large, fur-soled hind feet tell of its regular pathways, resting areas, and feeding sites. Dung pellets also help map out the animal's activities within its home range, which generally covers ten acres or less. In addition to normal, dry pellets containing indigestible waste the hare produces moist, glutinous droppings that it eats after depositing. This trait of reingesting feces, known as coprophagy, amounts to passing the same food through the gut twice. Practiced by both hares and rabbits, it achieves much the same purpose as processing food in more than one stomach, as the ruminant hoofed animals do. In both cases bacteria aid in breaking down plant material, producing important vitamins from otherwise indigestible woody tissues. While sign of snowshoe hares may be abundant in winter throughout the northern, or boreal, forests where the species ranges, the animal itself is difficult to see. Like other hares, it is primarily nocturnal. And if disturbed while abroad during the day, it freezes and blends into its surroundings, having replaced its brown summer coat for one of snowy white. The snowshoe hare is sometimes referred to as the varying hare. However, white-tailed jackrabbits and arctic hares also molt from brown to white with the coming of winter. The snowshoe hare is the smallest of the true hares, weighing just three pounds, while jackrabbits may reach five or six pounds and arctic hares as much as twelve.

37

MULE DEER, GLACIER NATIONAL PARK, MONTANA, JULY 1989

a coyote close, the way most people do. Now I sing the coyote people in with a song of need when I wish to tell them something.

Soon I will call them to see my lodge. First, though, I will make a medicine bundle with shells, dried serviceberries from a bush where a coyote sat eating his fill, and maybe the hollow wingbone of a loon for a flute. Then I will smudge it with the incense of sweetgrass and juniper. Then it will be right. Everyone needs a guide—a teacher, an extra source of help. Coyote will always be mine. In war. In love. In hunting and in finding my way. Coyote is my luck. Coyote shows me my place in the universe.

Now I am myself, a white man thinking over his place. I am a modern man trying to think of the most compelling reasons I can to save wildlife and places such as the Front. Trying to find the best answer I can for that stupid, troubling question: What good is a ———? Marmot. Goat. Turtle. Coyote. . . .

I will never converse with the living world as earlier people did, because I will never be so utterly sustained and renewed by it. I eat Cheezos and drive Ford pickup trucks. But I have walked alongside Kayapo Indians in the Amazon and pygmies in the Congo Basin who seemed able to intuit what an animal would do next almost as well as the animal itself. I've talked with shamans about the meaning of the light in wild cat eyes. And there are places in the world where I have lived immersed in creatures and conversed with them, if only because I had so many more of them than people for neighbors. Let me chant about them a little. They are the places I love best.

Mule deer (Odocoileus hemionus), found throughout the West, generally prefer more open habitat than white-tailed deer. They are also at home in more rugged terrain. In mountainous regions the males, or bucks, often spend part of the summer along the uppermost ridgelines and knolls. Bucks commonly band together in small bachelor groups until the approach of the autumn rutting season, when they become antler-clashing rivals for the company of females. Antlers are essentially outgrowths of bone—calcium phosphate—from the skull. The growth begins each spring, once food is in plentiful supply. Nourished by the skin covering known as velvet, which is engorged with blood vessels and coated with fine, silky hair, deer antlers may add up to one-third of an inch per day in length. Toward the latter part of summer the velvet dries out. The animal then begins to rub it off against trees and bushes, revealing the gleaming, hard headgear that comes into play during the mating season. Many biologists think that antlers are less important as weapons than as ornaments by which females can judge the general health and vigor of suitors. Sometime over winter, well after the end of the rut, the antlers become loose and eventually drop to the ground, where they serve as miniature mineral licks for an array of rodents.

ARCTIC FOX, ALASKA, JULY 1982

ALASKAN BROWN BEARS, BROOKS RIVER, ALASKA, JULY 1987

KODIAK BROWN BEAR, KODIAK ISLAND, ALASKA, JULY 1988

CHAPTER TWO

In Bear Country

GRIZZLIES ARE MUCH LIKE US: omnivorous, wide-ranging, and very adaptable; dexterous, curious, and playful. Highly intelligent, they learn quickly and keep learning over a long lifetime—up to thirty years in the wild. These are master mammals, supreme in their realm. They ought to make excellent teachers, if only because any mammal able to pick you up and eat you is going to have your undivided attention when it is around. Yet the fact that grizzlies can, and occasionally do, shred people is about all that some people are able to see out there. The bear might just as well be a dragon.

Time and again, I've watched tourists in Glacier National Park watch four- to five-hundred-pound grizzlies and describe them as weighing two, three, or four times that much and standing an impossible twelve to fifteen feet high. Megagrizz. All of us are stuck with whatever psychological process makes scary things tend to appear bigger than they really are. In addition, before most of us ever meet a real grizzly, we already have a passel of rip-snorting, gut-crunching, larger-than-life grizzlies roaming around in our heads for reference. They came with all the tales we have heard since childhood, and they have been there feeding on bad news ever since. When someone brings up the subject of grizzlies, it is usually as in: God, did you hear about that girl who got mauled by a grizzly over in Yellowstone? Or: I read where this hunter put eight shots into a grizzly's chest and it still kept charging. Headline grizz. Outdoor adventure magazine cover story grizz. Movie grizz. These are the ones we know best. Stories of peaceable, average-size, going-away-from-you grizz don't seem to stick in our memories well at all.

So we look straight at a wild grizzly bear and see the magnitude of our own fear. Then we think of that as the grizzly. Then, often, as throughout most of history, we kill it. In doing so we become bigger than life as well. We have slain the dragon, the outsize threat to us, our families, our flocks—the beast we named *Ursus arctos horribilis*. We have turned the bear into part of our own myth about ourselves.

South of the Canadian border the grizzly is listed as threatened. In the United States' best-known bear habitat, Yellowstone National Park, the population is only a few breeding females away from ruin. Across sections of the north country such patterns of decline are being played out all over again. We are seeing the great bear lose more of its place on the continent without yet having beheld the animal for what it is. Let me tell of a place where it is possible to see this sort of beast more clearly.

The McNeil River pours down through the tundra hills of the Alaska Peninsula and out into Kamishak Bay. Tides endlessly cover and uncover the river's wide delta, set between soaring, wave-cut headlands. Rain squalls and seals range up and down

The brown bear (Ursus arctos) is distributed throughout the northern hemisphere. In the Old World it is found from western Europe to the northern Japanese island Hokkaido. As most authorities now see it, North America has two subspecies. Ursus arctos middendorffi contains only the brown bears of Alaska's Kodiak Island and the two smaller islands next to it, Shuyak and Afognak. All the other brown bears of coastal Alaska and British Columbia are classified together with grizzlies as Ursus arctos horribilis. Evolving in isolation since toward the end of the last Ice Age, Kodiaks developed slightly wider, more inflated craniums than their mainland brethren. The Kodiak's great size—occasional specimens may weigh seventeen hundred pounds or more—is due primarily to an abundant food supply. Several different salmon-spawning runs take place each year in the islands' streams, and the moderate coastal climate supports a lush growth of berry bushes and other edible plants. Although continual harvesting of the biggest animals by trophy hunters has caused a decline in the average size of Kodiak bears over the years, the population appears to be thriving in terms of numbers. Portions of the Kodiak National Wildlife Refuge support a density of one bear every four hundred acres.

the coast while the vista of distant mountains and glaciers comes and goes in the mist. From the cold bay rises the perfect cone of a volcano, Augustine Island, its head wreathed in plumes from its own hot breath.

When the tide is out and the salmon are running in from the sea, brown bears patrol the mud flats and gravel bars. I once saw a big, solitary bear splashing after a school of fish in the shallows as two bald eagles kept pace a feather's length away on either side. The day was so bright the bear left a crystal wake; the wind was so strong the eagles never needed to flap their wings. They simply glided along at bear speed, hoping to share in the feast. They did.

The fishing is even better about half an hour's walk upriver, where the water falls over a series of ledges. A few salmon may be able to make it all the way to the top in one rocketing effort. Far more are washed back at some point to collect in eddies along the whitewater cascade, gathering strength for their next surge. Bears, meanwhile, collect among the milling, vaulting, egg-laden swimmers. Late in July, on the final day of my most recent visit to McNeil, there were fifty-eight bears at the cascade, all within a stretch of little more than two hundred yards. That was a record for McNeil at the time, but to see twenty to thirty bears at once is quite ordinary there. In fact, this is one of the largest known brown bear congregations on the globe. To safeguard the spectacular gathering of big airborne fish and shaggy wild anglers, Alaska designated a strip of land between the delta and a point well upstream of the cascade as the McNeil River State Game Sanctuary late in the 1970s. Its 83,840 acres are managed by the Alaska Department of Fish and Game.

No two McNeil bears seem to use quite the same fishing techniques. There are biters that snap their jaws at passing fish, often catching them in midair; swipers that field their prey with a forepaw; plungers that leap off midstream boulders after resting salmon; surface snorkelers; deep-divers that paddle around completely submerged like colossal otters; fatal embracers that stand or sit in a pool and try to clutch to their body any fish that bumps into them; pin-them-on-the-bottomers; and gallop-around-after-everythingers. The last are usually younger animals and, not surprisingly, the least successful. Then there are the bears given to stealing someone else's fish. And such fish-snatchers can be divided into those that rely on stealth and those that use intimidation.

Dominant bears don't claim other bears' fish outright all that often. They regularly claim the best fishing spots when they arrive, though, forcing other bears away through threats or, less commonly, bites and blows. A displaced bear may turn around and take over a lesser bear's spot, and so on down the ranks to the smallest gallop-around-after-everythinger. Females with cubs are concerned with finding fishing sites that their offspring can safely reach through the churning current. If the cubs are too young to do more than wait on shore, the mother settles for the best spot from which she can keep a close watch on her crew. She must take care that they don't get too near roiling water as they roughhouse and explore. More importantly, she must guard them against large, aggressive bears.

ALASKAN BROWN BEAR, MCNEIL FALLS, ALASKA, JULY 1984

SEA OTTER, ALTHORP INLET, ALASKA, NOVEMBER 1987

It soon becomes clear to the visitor that this scene represents far more than a bunch of bears angling for fish. It is an assortment of individuals of differing size, age, experience, social rank, and temperament all trying to figure out how to get along in a crowd—a very large crowd for this normally rather solitary species.

The brown bear, *Ursus arctos*, is distributed throughout much of the northern hemisphere. Here on the Alaska Peninsula are many of the biggest specimens of all, occasionally reaching three-quarters of a ton or more. Their size is matched only by those on nearby Kodiak Island, just across the Shelikof Strait, and on the Soviet Union's Kamchatka Peninsula, which lies near the end of the arc formed by the Alaska Peninsula and the Aleutian chain. It is no coincidence that all three areas are rich in several species of salmon. Spawning runs follow one after another through the warm months.

The brown bears of the Kodiak archipelago, commonly called Kodiaks, are now classified as the subspecies *Ursus arctos middendorffi*. All the other brown bears of the Alaskan coastal region, often termed brownies or big brown bears, are placed in the subspecies *Ursus arctos horribilis*. This is the same subspecies to which grizzlies belong. As a rule grizzlies have slightly longer claws and more silver-tipped fur than brownies do. Grizzlies also tend to occupy more open habitats than brownies. But the two varieties—biologists prefer the term ecotypes—grade into one another so gradually that no one can truly say where grizzlies end and brownies begin. The rule of thumb is that those found within seventy-five miles of the coast are brownies, while any brown bear east of that line must be a grizzly. Yes, it is arbitrary, not to mention confusing. But that is our problem, not the bears'.

Early in each salmon run the fish are relatively few, strong, and agile, and the bears have to work fairly hard for a meal. More and more salmon arrive as the run progresses, until you could practically walk across their backs in some channels. At the end of a day's fishing many a big-bellied bear is simply biting out the piece of the salmon's head containing the brain, then slitting the belly with a single, precise stroke of one four-inch-long claw to lick out the eggs—the caviar. The rest is discarded and quickly disappears beneath the hunched wings of gulls, ravens, and scavenging bald eagles.

The bears remind me what it must have been like with Indians at a buffalo jump when times were good. Having stampeded an entire bison herd off a cliff edge, a well-fed Indian band might take only the humps and tongues from the bodies piled below. Toward the end of a run brownies grow more picky than ever as the salmon turn soft and sluggish and begin to lose their flavor. The fish, after all, are on a sort of death march, with their tissues programmed to fall apart after spawning. By midsummer a number of bears already look waddling plump, as if they could crawl into a den right then and live until spring on their own salmon-spawned layers of fat.

Obviously there is no shortage of protein for these coastal bears as long as they don't have to spend too much time fighting others to get at it. They seldom do. Bears are opportunists, adapted to take full advantage of concentrated, seasonally abun-

The sea otter (Enhydra lutris) is the largest of the mustelid, or weasel, family and the only truly sea-going member, though the river otter (Lutra canadensis) may be seen in saltwater estuaries and bays. The sea otter is also the only marine mammal that qualifies as a regular tool-user. Floating on its back and holding a rock in its paw, it pounds open molluscs that it has gathered while diving, using its chest for a table. This thirty- to one-hundred-pound, web-footed carnivore also takes crabs and sea urchins. After sea otter populations were decimated by fur hunters around the start of the century, urchin populations exploded and began devastating the kelp beds off California. Since sea otters were given protection they have recovered along the coast south of Monterey and in the Aleutian Island chain. Nevertheless they remain few in number and extremely vulnerable to spills of oil and other contaminants.

47

WALRUS, ROUND ISLAND,
ALASKA, JULY 1987

dant resources such as salmon. That adaptation includes an ability to dampen the level of aggression that normally keeps them apart in separate home ranges. Their sense of critical space—the fight-or-flight distance—shrinks accordingly. Spanish colonists saw the same sort of behavior when California's golden grizzlies gathered by the score to banquet on the carcasses of beached whales. The sight of several bears side by side tugging meat off a bison carcass in Yellowstone recalls the days—buffalo jump days—when North America had perhaps one hundred thousand or more grizzlies to go with its millions upon millions of bison. Even grizzlies gathering in a prime patch of ripe berries become more mellow than usual toward one another, though this is not always so obvious.

As bears settle in at a get-together and begin to fill their bellies their dispositions continue to improve. Whose wouldn't? I mean, after downing three helpings of Thanksgiving Day turkey with all the trimmings plus pie, how much do you feel like racing around and giving everyone a hard time? Along salmon streams the bears' tolerance extends to eagles, foxes, and other hunters and scavengers drawn by the bounty. Sometimes wolves fish between the bears. I once saw a deer eating salmon carcasses next to a bear, presumably for salts. Such tolerance is also shown humans.

Wildlife enthusiasts have been treated to any number of spectacular closeup photographs of brown bears catching salmon. Many of the best come from McNeil. However, the photographers seldom turn their lenses around to reveal the situation that allowed them such intimate access. Too bad. The *horribilis*-human relationship at McNeil is equally spectacular in its own way, especially since so many people would never imagine just how closely the two species can coexist.

The scene behind the camera looks like this: Down at the delta's edge is the Department of Fish and Game biologists' shack; next to that is the visitors' camp with a wooden cookshack and an adjoining meadow where tents may be pitched amid the wildflowers, rustling rodents, and curious foxes. The visitors are chosen by lottery from a list of applicants, which includes a large proportion of foreigners, for McNeil has a growing international reputation. Most arrive by float plane. Each morning no more than ten people, accompanied by a department biologist, proceed up to the cascade. They always follow the same trail and arrive at the same early hour at the same small section of riverbank a few dozen feet from the water's edge. The upper part is simply a rock ledge, marked off from the surrounding grass and sedge hummocks by a thin strip of wood on the ground. The lower part is a shallow cave just beneath the ledge. From these two positions the visitors watch bears all day, then depart as a group in the evening, retracing the trail back to camp.

"Unpredictable" is one of the labels we've stuck *horribilis* with. The awesome, unpredictable grizzly. The brown bear, huge and unpredictable. Even educational material passes along these stock phrases. What unpredictable really means is that this mammal no longer relies much upon simple stereotypical behavior to survive. It is anything but a slave to instinct. A bear's next move depends upon a combination of its mood at the moment, the knowledge it has accumulated up to that point, and a

Weighing more than three thousand pounds in the case of big adult males, the walrus (Odobenus rosmarus) comes in two subspecies: divergens, *the Pacific walrus, and* rosmarus, *the slightly smaller Atlantic walrus. Adapted to life in arctic waters, this marine mammal has a wrinkled skin up to two inches thick over layers of insulating blubber. It may dive three hundred feet down in search of its chief food, shellfish, which it senses and pries loose with the aid of hundreds of stout bristles that cover its muzzle like a moustache. Both sexes carry tusks that are modified canine teeth. Although they may be used to rake shellfish off the bottom at times, this is probably not their chief function, as was long believed. Up to two or even three feet long, the tusks are of more critical importance in dominance battles and also in defense against such predators as polar bears. In addition they serve as hooks that help the animal haul itself up onto ice floes. Now and then a male turns to feeding on carrion or even to hunting seals and small whales, including narwhals, putting its canine teeth to work in yet another way. It is a reminder that walrus represent a carnivore line closely related to eared seals. The ivory from their tusks has just recently risen sharply in value, as many countries banned elephant ivory to protect Africa's heavily poached pachyderms.*

49

Of the world's seventy-seven cetacean species, forty-seven can be found in the waters surrounding the North American continent and Hawaii. That includes all six species in the rorqual, or furrow-throated, whale family. The humpback (Megaptera novaeangliae) is perhaps the most commonly seen representative. Other rorquals are the Bryde's whale, minke, fin, sei, and the largest mammal, the blue whale. Humpbacks occur off both coasts. In the Pacific some spend the winter, which is the breeding and birthing period, off Mexico and around Hawaii, where a special marine preserve has been established to help protect them. During spring they begin moving north toward Alaska's arctic and subarctic waters. Some Atlantic populations winter off the Bahamas and migrate toward Newfoundland, Labrador, and Greenland in the warmer months. A humpback whale may grow to a length of fifty-two feet and weigh an equal number of tons—about fifty-one—with females being slightly larger than males.

host of other variables—possibly including an ability to make judgments. Rather than calling bears unpredictable, we could just as fairly call them smart or creative. But we have reserved those terms for describing ourselves. And we are one of the least predictable creatures ever invented.

The human reaction upon meeting a backcountry bear is a perfect example. Where one person might go racing away screaming, the next might freeze, fall down, blow a whistle, or climb a tree. And the next might walk right up to the beast instead, maybe hoping to take a picture. Or to scratch a big teddy bear behind the ears. Or to blast it with a shotgun. McNeil works especially well because the bears, for once, can tell what the humans are going to be doing from one minute to the next.

How do these bears act, then? The answer is that they more or less ignore the humans. At times they do it with deliberation. A direct stare being an almost universally recognized form of threat among mammals, the bears are very careful to avoid looking right at the people when passing close by. Although they may come within inches of the people space, and although nothing stands between them and the people but thin air, the bears know exactly where the border is and make no attempt to cross it. Why should they? We never harm them. We never try to take anybody's fishing spot. We seem happy to hang out all day in a spot with no fish whatsoever, reared up on two legs like skinny little bears endlessly looking for something.

For the human observer McNeil is the next best thing to being invisible and magically transported into a world of giants. With the deep music and dancing of the water, the wheeling birds, the hulking, shaggy shapes of bears moving on all sides, you hum with a pitch of wonder that you may not have experienced before. At first fear is part of it. Then the fear slowly and surely sweeps away, and you are finally free to see bears just as bears, going about their lives. Before long you sense what an anthropologist must feel like when discovering a new tribe.

As soon as you start picking up some of the body language, you find yourself getting to know each bear as a personality, or, more properly, a bearality. Bearality traits—*Ursus* versions of shy, bold, easygoing, edgy, cautious, adventurous—provide further insight into why we have had so much trouble understanding these animals. An individual bear doesn't seem all that unpredictable; not once you've become familiar with its particular bearality. The confusion begins when you generalize from any single individual to say that bears will do this or bears will do that. Some of them are bound to start proving you wrong, because the range of bearalities is so wonderfully wide.

But no matter how hard you try to peer around the next corner, you never can be exactly sure what life has in store. One afternoon a subadult bear ran by so close to me that its fur brushed my knee. I don't think it noticed, or cared. It was too busy looking over its shoulder at the older bear chasing it. On a different day a big female that had been squabbling with another over a loose fish suddenly stood up about ten feet from my perch in the shallow cave and began to growl. Fish blood was all over her mouth. River water still dripped off the ridges of her hair. Soon she was roaring.

HUMPBACK WHALE, SOUTHEAST ALASKA, AUGUST 1989

TUFTED PUFFIN, PRIBILOF ISLANDS,
ALASKA, MAY 1989

Her eyes were wide, showing way too much white. Her muzzle was wrinkling with tensed muscles. Saliva began spilling out between her teeth and flying in every direction as she swung her head.

Didn't I know the signs of a coming explosion by now? Hadn't I been watching sparring matches break out in the cascade and wondering how barrel-shaped beasts of that size could move as fast as cats? Hadn't I seen one half-ton McNeil bear pick another up with its jaws and flip it over its shoulder?

She took a step closer, went down on all fours, then stood up again and spun from side to side, roaring louder the whole time. She dropped and ran two yards one way, three yards the other way. A yard closer. Roaring wild. Up again, staring at me, away, back toward me. My thoughts flashed back to times I'd blundered much too close to bears in Montana—bears that came racing toward me, roaring. And all I could think now was: I knew McNeil was too good to be true. We'd just been riding on dumb luck until now. Look at her. *Look at her!* Eight hundred pounds of bear was about to lose its mind and tear into anything stupid enough to still be close by, and that's exactly where I was—cornered in the cave mouth like a Cro-Magnon, except that he would at least have had a spear.

Suddenly the bear bounded upslope from the edge of the cave toward the upper ledge where most of the other visitors and the state biologist were, though I couldn't see them. I heard more roaring, expecting it to be followed by either a scream or a gunshot, for the biologist always carried a weapon just in case. I had been told that no bear had ever been killed at the cascade and that no person had ever been injured. This was surely going to be the first time for one or the other, I thought.

But there were no shots, no screams. The bear left. Soon she was back fishing. And later, talking it over with the other adrenalized visitors, I realized that what I had thought was a bear working itself up into an uncontrollable rage over a lost fish was in fact a mother that had looked up and noticed that her cubs were missing. Her problem was that she couldn't see them, and a lot of other big bears were much too close for her comfort. She was plenty upset, but her anger was neither out of control nor directed toward us.

The biologist, a woman, had patrolled the edge of the people space and calmly talked to the bear the way most of the biologists do when a bear in an agitated state comes too near. "Okay. Okay. That's close enough. Come on, back off a little. Your cubs are right over there, now. Come on, now. That's a girl. Easy. Okay. Okay."

As I said, McNeil is the *next* best thing to being invisible. Humans are a definite presence there. Sometimes a subordinate bear being harried by a dominant one will even run around to the opposite side of the people space and use it as a kind of barrier. Halfway through a rainy afternoon a cub actually breached the people space, running between people's legs to hide from a subadult. That worked. But then mother came looking for it. Now what? As it turned out, the mother was known for her even temper. She was the kind that would lie on her back at the very border of the people ledge to nurse and play with her offspring. I had the impression that she

Using its short, stout, tapered wings to "fly" underwater much as penguins do, the tufted puffin (Fratercula cirrhata) chases prey through Pacific waters. It hunts no more than one hundred feet down as a rule, but it can range almost twice as deep. Like other puffin species, it subsists mainly on fish and secondarily on squid and shrimp. Its diet also includes molluscs and sea urchins. This may be related to the fact that it ranges farther south than other puffins. Tufted puffins breed in colonies along the coasts of Siberia, Alaska, and British Columbia, with a few nesting on California cliffs. They winter from southern Alaska to southern California, often remaining far out at sea for months at a time. During this period the long ivory white tufts, or plumes, that curve back from above the eyes are gone, along with the white coloration of the face. These characteristic traits reappear in the spring molt, in preparation for the breeding season.

53

liked our company, though it may have been mainly that the people space was a safe zone with no big bears in it for her to worry about. In any case she waited patiently until her baby emerged from the thicket of people legs, nuzzled it, and went on about her business.

Key misconceptions have always been that brownies and grizzlies attack people out of some primal urge to tear into whatever confronts them, or else that they view humans primarily as food, or both. Monster motives, in other words. But a surprising number of *horribilis* are almost entirely vegetarian. Besides, bears usually run away from humans in the backcountry. When a bear does rush a human, more often than not it is only a bluff. Typically the bear doesn't want to catch us and eat us. It wants either to get away or make *us* go away. Bears view people as potential threats to themselves, their cubs, or their home ranges. This is more or less how they view other bears. They relate to us within the context of bear social behavior, not as predators confronting prey. This isn't especially reassuring, to be sure, since bears chase, cuff, chew, kill, and sometimes eat other bears.

The saying of Pogo, the cartoon opossum, "We have met the enemy and he is us," was meant to describe the human condition. To some extent it applies to other dominant species at the top of the food chain as well. In wild communities the one animal a grizzly or brownie has to beware of has always been another of its own kind. At McNeil, a common ground, the bears treat both humans and each other more deferentially than usual. In certain respects, as illustrated by the incident of the mother waiting for her cub to come out from between the people, they treat humans with *more* consideration than they would show toward other bears. I'm convinced that somewhat the same consideration is being granted us in crowded parks and preserves inhabited by big bears that see, hear, or at least scent people fairly often throughout the day; the bears would not accept so many strange bears so close. For that matter, I've found examples of grizzlies making successful use of natural habitats close to homes and ranches by carefully avoiding critical people spaces there.

When I look at one of these animals now, I still see something with enormous strength and an explosive range of moods. But having been to McNeil, I can also see more clearly a powerful mind out there roaming the countryside. It is quite capable of learning how to live with our presence today. The question, as we extend that presence through more and more of the remaining wildlands, is whether we will be able to learn anything at all from the bear.

One of the most important lessons that this giant has to teach us has to do with respect. Our psyches hardly take kindly to lessons in how to defer to others. But those are the lessons we most need, I think, for respect is not a diminishing but an opening up—the essential first step toward understanding. The flight of antelope across sagebrush hills or the vertical skills of a mountain goat on an icy peak should tell us clearly enough to ease off our claim to total dominion and to leave room for nature to keep working wonders. Sometimes, though, it takes a species on the order of a great brown bear to make us stand back and think twice about what our next

DALL'S SHEEP, ALASKA RANGE, ALASKA, SEPTEMBER 1986

POLAR BEAR, MANITOBA, NOVEMBER 1983

move should be. If we want to act proud, let it be for saving and sharing a place such as McNeil.

Setting aside the McNeil River State Game Sanctuary proved to be only the first stage of protecting its wildlife, however. Too many guides and hunters began stalking the edge of the narrow strip for bears coming and going around the cascade, and the animals' numbers began to decrease. In addition there were problems with commercial trawlers taking more than their allotted salmon quota from the bay, depleting the stocks of fish before they could continue upstream to spawn. Finally growing recreational use of the surrounding area, both by private individuals and by lodges catering to fishermen and naturalists, led to more human food and garbage becoming available to passing bears. As usual this turned good bears into bears with what we consider bad habits, raiding campsites and backpacks and scaring off people.

To deal with the first concern Alaska closed the bear hunting season on state lands to the south between the sanctuary and Katmai National Park, in effect giving the brownies a greatly expanded refuge. The overfishing issue was ironed out through the Fish and Game Department's commercial fisheries division. Then the Fish and Game Department, the Department of Natural Resources, and the National Park Service all got together to discuss how to handle recreation on lands adjoining the sanctuary. They decided that the same sort of bear problems were developing there that had already occurred in national parks. And since the National Park Service had been working long and hard to find solutions—from improved garbage disposal to better public education—it was the logical agency to direct the management of what might be called the greater McNeil River area. This includes both state lands to the south of McNeil now protected from hunting and state lands around Kamishak Bay where hunting is one of the many outdoor activities that draw increasing numbers of people each year.

Alaska's novel cooperative agreement for McNeil is still in the draft stages. But the officials I spoke with see no major obstacles to its completion. In fact, they may expand the entire protection package to still more of the countryside near McNeil in the future. Similarly, in the greater Yellowstone ecosystem, concern for the isolated and seriously threatened population of grizzlies has caused a welter of state and federal bureaucracies to look beyond the narrow boundaries of their own traditional turf, join together, and begin treating the area as a single living resource. To save a creature as many-sided as the great bear, we have to do a great many things right. In this sense *Ursus arctos horribilis* is proving to be one of the leading conservationists of our time.

That the great bear remains a stong presence in a landscape means the whole countryside is strong. Intact. Where this animal drinks, chances are the waters still run sweet. Where it breathes, the air will be clean and bright. Where the great bear still has room to go about its affairs, so can all the smaller beasts that need homes and space and a little respect. And that part of the kingdom will still be good enough, wild enough, big enough, free enough for us.

Polar bears (Ursus maritimus) *are the size of the larger brown bears, averaging nine hundred to eleven hundred pounds. The brown bear line gave rise to polar bears perhaps a hundred thousand years ago, and the two different-looking species are still close enough genetically that they have interbred and produced fertile offspring in zoos. The distinctive white to creamy yellow fur of polar bears has an obvious value as camouflage when the predator is stalking its prime food source—seals—across the ice floes. Some observers claim that a polar bear will even cover its black nose with a white paw when lurking by a seal's breathing hole. While the polar bear hunted marine mammals, Eskimos hunted the sea bear for its meat and fur. Experience taught the Eskimos not to consume the liver, which contains toxic concentrations of vitamin A. Once airplanes and snow machines made this bear accessible to trophy hunters as well as to natives, polar bear populations underwent substantial declines. Today the animals are protected by an international agreement that allows only traditional hunting by native peoples of the Soviet Union and North America.*

57

PRONGHORN, UTAH, NOVEMBER 1989

KINGSNAKE, SIERRA NEVADA, CALIFORNIA, AUGUST 1989

DESERT KIT FOX,
ARIZONA, JUNE 1985

CHAPTER THREE

The Big Lonesome

To the Greeks the virgin huntress Artemis was the goddess of wild nature. Many worshipped her as the Mistress of Animals. A great temple built in her honor by Croesus, the outrageously rich king of Lydia, was one of the Seven Wonders of the World. Another of the Seven Wonders was the original Mausoleum, built by the queen of ancient Caria in Asia Minor during the fourth century B.C. to entomb her husband, Mausolus. Called Artemisia, after Artemis, the queen was also renowned for her studies of medicine and botany. More than two millennia later, her name was honored by being given to a genus of plants in the large and diverse family that includes sunflowers and asters. Some *Artemisia* are soft-stemmed, or herbaceous. The rest are shrubs with woody stems. On this continent they go by the name of sagebrush.

I'd been traveling out there for weeks on end through the windy, silver-green sagebrush sea, rolling along past bullet-riddled road signs with my car windows down and the radio up and all the blue sky and stars in the world overhead. And the range just kept opening ahead that way—so free and endless, I had a coyote feeling building up inside like I didn't know whether to sing for joy or cry for myself. Time to slow down a little, I figured; maybe stick around one place for a spell.

Right around Vya wouldn't be bad. I could hunker down here in Nevada's northwestern corner and keep an eye on a few sage grouse. It was April, and these birds were deep into their ceremonies of courtship and mating like some remarkable dryland tribe. Each breeding ground, referred to as a lek, is generally chosen in habitat where the sagebrush is fairly low and scattered so that the birds have a good view of their immediate surroundings, including one another. Some leks contain a handful of males. A few around Vya hold close to two hundred, gathering each morning in the cool gray light that precedes the dawn.

Having begun sorting out a dominance hierarchy in the waning weeks of winter, the male groups by now had a distinct arrangement on the lek. The periphery of each arena I observed was occupied by the lowest-ranking males. Then came a sort of inner hub of more dominant animals. In the center of that strutted the kingpin, the master cock.

These are the largest of the various grouse on the continent. In their mating rituals, they make themselves larger yet by spreading stiff, turkeylike fans of tailfeathers; elevating long, white, hairlike neck feathers; expanding the bright yellow combs over

The kit fox (Vulpes macrotis) *inhabits the dry sagebrush country of the Great Basin, along with the still more arid Sonoran, Mojave, and Chihuahuan deserts of the American Southwest. Its notably large ears help radiate excess body heat. They also aid this fox in its search for prey. It chiefly hunts rodents such as pocket mice, voles, and kangaroo rats, but it will take snakes, lizards, birds, and insects. For the most part the kit fox stalks at night, spending the day in an underground burrow, which may be one it has dug itself or one left by a badger or a prairie dog. Massive predator poisoning campaigns directed chiefly against the coyote all but exterminated the kit fox, while the coyote soon learned to avoid many types of bait and traps. Since the use of strychnine, sodium cyanide, thallium sulfate, and the still more lethal biocide called Compound 1080—sodium monofluoroacetate—was banned on public lands during the early 1970s, the kit fox has made a modest comeback. Some night under a desert moon, then, between howls of coyotes, you might detect a yipping so high-pitched it has been compared to the chattering of a squirrel. This is the voice of the kit fox, smallest of all the canids on the continent at three to seven pounds.*

The black bear (Ursus americanus) still has one of the broadest ranges of all the continent's large mammals. Adaptable and omnivorous, it is equally at home in Alaska's Glacier Bay area, the dry hills of northern Mexico, or rural areas of the long-settled East Coast. Some have been found making winter dens in suburban woodlots and even under porches in populous New Jersey. Unlike their larger relative, the brown bear, which merely snoozes in its den and may occasionally roam outside during midwinter thaws, black bears become truly dormant, lowering their metabolic rate sharply and becoming so sluggish that they cannot be roused from sleep. Female black bears average about 150 pounds and males twice as much. A few specimens reach 600 pounds or so, larger than many grizzlies. In their foraging, black bears are opportunists with strong individual preferences and habits. They have been seen chasing large animals from mountain goats to deer, and they will readily take the young of ungulates during spring. Yet many black bears seldom taste red meat except in the form of scavenged carrion. The main source of animal protein for nearly all black bears consists of insects and their larvae, obtained by tearing apart rotting logs and overturning stones. And, in terms of sheer volume, most of the black bear's diet consists of vegetation, from sprouting grass and tubers to nuts and berries. Every so often the black bear may add the contents of a hiker's backpack.

the eyes; and pumping up the thick, white air sac—an extension of the esophagus—on the chest. They stalk stiffly about, giving off loud, pneumatic sounds as the air sacs suddenly empty into two yellow patches of bare breast skin, which causes them to inflate and just as suddenly collapse with a "Whop! Whop!" Sheer organic fireworks. The locals call it "booming."

Drawn by this display, females fly into the lek singly or in small groups, and work their way past strutting males toward the very hub. There the master cock performs about 90 percent of the actual breeding. Males whose territories lie close to his occasionally get some of the overflow when a number of hens show up at once. Only on the rarest of occasions does a cock toward the outer edge succeed in distracting an incoming hen and copulating with her, though he will be there booming every single morning until the sun stands above the horizon, and again each evening, and, often, on through the night when the moon is full from late February into April.

One morning the cocks at a lek that encompassed the side of a low, rounded knoll succeeded in attracting both a fair number of hens and a solitary antelope. This yearling male would walk a few feet, pause, stare at a bird, then angle off toward a different one. It might crane its neck toward the strutting, booming grouse and break into an antelope jig, or trot on a few more feet to stare at the next bird. For their part the grouse didn't appear to be paying much attention to the hoofed creature, though more fights than usual erupted as males making way for the antelope crossed into neighboring territories. Then I turned away to check on a second antelope across a gully from the lek, and when I turned back, all I saw was the yearling standing alone on a slope of shrubs and basalt rubble with glimmering flecks of obsidian. Of the eighty-some cocks that had been spread across that terrain in the breaking light, spiky tail fans aglow like big thistles among the brush, I could not find one. Even the horned larks that had been shouting about the nearby territories they owned had gone quiet.

Shading my eyes, I eventually made out a cock crouched low among the phlox blossoms. He began to rise and spread his tail fan. Abruptly he deflated back into a mottled brown huddle of feathers. His head, touching the ground, lay cocked to one side, one eye gazing skyward. I followed his line of sight: it was not the antelope that had shrunk these grouse. It was a pair of golden eagles circling high overhead.

The eagles widened their circle until they were lost in the distance. One by one the grouse puffed up into view again. The antelope took another ten minutes to satisfy its curiosity and then rambled on east, its silhouette melting into the ascending ball of the sun. Soon afterwards groups of cocks began launching themselves from the breeding grounds, flying off to begin a morning meal. By the hour most humans begin their day, the lek and the hills around it were hushed and motionless save for the wind. Oh, there were still ants and black bombardier beetles scuttling under the sagebrush canopy among kangaroo rat tracks, coyote droppings, arrowhead fragments and spent metal cartridge cases, shed snake skins and mule deer antlers, pawed-out clumps of dried bunchgrass telling of heavy feeding by wild horses over

BLACK BEAR, GLACIER BAY, ALASKA, MAY 1989

SNOWY EGRET, BRIGANTINE NATIONAL WILDLIFE REFUGE, NEW JERSEY, MAY 1989

the past winter, and the old hoof scrape of a buck antelope marking its territory. And, in the distance, some tourists barreling by in a plume of dust on their way to Vegas or the California coast were probably thinking, "My God, it's empty way out here. What a wasteland."

Tough and adapted to extremes, sagebrush covers a little better than one out of every twelve acres in the Lower 48. The Great Basin, that immensity between the Rockies and the Sierra with no outlet to the sea, is practically made of the stuff. So are the Columbia Plateau, Colorado Plateau, and Wyoming Basin. Northern Mexico has a share. Even streaks of Alberta and British Columbia give off its bittersweet scent.

Most of these landscapes are high—four thousand feet or more above sea level—and thirsty, averaging only eight to twelve inches of rainfall a year. Summers are long and scorching. Winters are long and hard-frozen. Some call this realm our continent's cold desert, or the high desert. Others speak of the shrub steppe, a fancy name for scrublands. I like American outback. What we're really talking about is the big lonesome heart of the West.

Popular lore sometimes makes it seem as though the cowboy way of life that developed here is all about riding and roping, boots and saddles and big hats and such. In the end, though, it's all about the relationships between shrubs, grasses, and water. So is the survival of wildlife. And nine-tenths of this vast domain is actually your property and mine—public land. Most of it is administered by the Bureau of Land Management (BLM), which leases grazing rights to ranchers. But this is still our spread, our holdings, and I like to think of the native fauna as our wild stock. So it becomes important to have some sort of handle on basic sagebrush ecology—some idea of how the lean land underlying our richest frontier mythology works.

Under pristine conditions this arid range sprawling across the western interior is anything but a wasteland. It is a finely balanced mosaic of bushes and grasses—neither shrubfield nor grass prairie, but a dynamic mixture of the two in which very little is wasted.

For sage grouse *Artemisia* is virtually the only food taken through the cold months. The animals are built from sagebrush, and they taste like it; they carry the fragrance around in their muscles and blood. The same holds for many black-tailed jackrabbits. A related species, the little known pygmy rabbit, which resembles a diminutive cottontail rabbit with a dark tail, is found almost exclusively in sagebrush habitat. Sage sparrows, sage thrashers, sagebrush voles, and sagebrush lizards are obviously tied to the shrub. Bobcats, kit foxes, Brewer's sparrows, western fence lizards, rattlesnakes, and dozens of other species rely upon sagebrush as well—if not for food, then for nesting habitat, shelter, or at least shade, a crucial requirement during high desert summers.

On the other hand, the volatile oils that give sagebrush its unmistakable tang make the plant unpalatable to most hoofed animals and hard for them to digest. The exception is the pronghorn, sole member of the Antilocapridae family, and unrelated to the African or Asian species called antelope. That may be because it is the only

65

wild ungulate that evolved here alongside sagebrush rather than arising in Eurasia and migrating to the New World across Beringia during the Ice Age.

Elk and mule deer would rather eat shrubs other than sagebrush if they have a choice. So would bighorn sheep, once common throughout many of the high desert's mountain ranges. So, too, would the most recent immigrants from Eurasia: cattle and sheep. And all the hoofed animals, pronghorn included, depend primarily on grasses, not shrubs, during the crucial spring growing season, as well as at various other times throughout the year.

As the owners of such pastures, we should be aware that the grasses of the cold desert are species known as bunchgrasses, so called because each plant grows as a separate clump of stalks, rather than spreading to form a continuous grassy turf. Because the little precipitation that the cold desert enjoys comes mainly as snow, western bunchgrasses are designed by nature to shoot up and produce seed before the last meltwater is baked out of the soil—usually by the end of June. Nearly all of the energy stored in their root systems is thrown into this spring effort. If wild—or domestic—animals graze the bunchgrasses back down once or twice during the growing period, there might be enough reserves left for one more try. Hit them any harder, though, and it could be the last anyone will see of these plants, particularly if they were munched down the previous year or two. The cold desert will claim them as part of its dust.

In the Great Plains, by contrast, spring rains are followed by summer thundershowers, providing enough moisture to sustain growth and ripening through the warm months. Graze down true prairie grasses and they come right back up like your lawn, resprouting from growth nodes along rhizomes, or runners, that spread horizontally just beneath the surface. Unlike bunchgrasses, these rhizomatous grasses are extremely well-adapted to resist the effects of grazing and trampling by hoofs. In fact, they flourish under pressure. It is only what you would expect of plants that co-evolved with bison herds, which came rumbling through the landscape like a geologic force, along with the majority of the continent's elk and mule deer.

Sagebrush country never held large herds of buffalo. Nor did it sustain high densities of any other hoofed animals. The staple food of the Paiute, Shoshone, and Bannock Indians living there was jackrabbits, supplemented by ground squirrels, grasshoppers, ant eggs, and the seeds of Indian ricegrass and Basin wild rye. Nevertheless, portions of the sagebrush steppe looked almost as promising as the Great Plains to early white stockmen. Just how promising is hard for us to appreciate today. For the veneer of lush native grass growth that once existed across the cold desert was quickly stripped off—and kept off—by the animals the stockmen trailed in. Therein lies the real saga of the West.

The early cowboys and sheepherders were not self-sufficient individuals intent on carving a home out of the frontier. They were, for the most part, migratory corporate employees driving herds of tremendous size back and forth across the wide open land. That livestock was the property of large business interests based mainly in the

EASTERN COTTONTAIL RABBIT, NEW YORK, MAY 1988

East Coast and Europe, taking advantage of what looked to be half a continent of free pasture. Nobody owned the West. Or else everybody did. It was strictly a get-there-first-and-grab-the-grass contest between colonists.

Before the snowbound winter of 1889 to 1890, when herders tore the thatched roofs off their huts to feed starving beasts, sagebrush country stockmen never even stopped to put up hay. They used the range year-round without letup. As early as 1910 a congressional report described serious abuse of western rangelands. Portions of Utah pastures were described as grazed down to dirt and eroding well before the turn of the century. Wyoming alone once held more than half as many tame sheep as the entire United States does today. In southeastern Oregon biologists at the Hart Mountain National Antelope Refuge explained to me how they currently fine-tune the movements of two thousand cattle to prevent overuse. As late as 1930 there were twenty thousand cows and one hundred thousand domestic sheep, plus thousands of wild horses, munching away in the Hart Mountain area. Earlier, single bands containing up to half a million sheep had worked their way through that same country.

Having never sustained big herds of wild ungulates, the arid steppe's native plant communities simply could not adjust to such numbers of livestock. However, to the torn, trampled, and increasingly bare ground left in the wake of those herds came plant species that could handle the pressure because they, like livestock, evolved in Eurasia: tumbleweed, beloved of western songwriters and moviemakers, but more accurately called Russian thistle; tumble mustard, rolled in from the Mediterranean; medusahead, from the Asian steppe and slightly poisonous; halogeton, also poisonous (archeologists note that it showed up in Iranian settlements about the time wild sheep and goats were first domesticated); cheatgrass, more common today than any grass native to sagebrush country. In springtime you'll see hillsides of this Mediterranean annual greened up like rolling fields of young grain. By June, if not earlier, it will have cheated on its promise, offering dry mouthfuls of sharp seeds with little nutritional value. In an effort to provide more livestock forage on deteriorating ranges, managers seeded millions upon millions of acres with grass—not native grass but crested wheatgrass, yet another import from the steppes of Asia.

One native, however, has prospered as never before under the cowboys' reign: sagebrush itself. On many a hillside it is about the only plant left that really belongs there. It likes things hard. It knows all about thirsty. An extensive system of fine lateral roots in the upper soil and a thick central root that penetrates much deeper levels allow the larger varieties of sagebrush to extract minerals and water from a subterranean area the size of a house. *Artemisia* moves in as the native grasses and forbs—a collective term for herbs and wildflowers—are eaten out. And most animals would rather keep on searching for what's left of those plants than take another bite of the pungent silver-green sagebrush closing in from all sides. The one thing that will knock woody shrubs back and encourage grass growth instead is natural fire. Sagebrush therefore owes us thanks for a century's worth of efforts to suppress fires in the misguided belief that this would help preserve rangelands.

BIGHORN SHEEP AND ELK, YELLOWSTONE NATIONAL PARK, WYOMING, JANUARY 1989

RATTLESNAKE, COLUMBIA PLATEAU, WASHINGTON, MARCH 1989

In battling the spread of sagebrush ranchers and public land managers tore the stuff out with tractors, grubbed it up by hand, and strung giant chains between bulldozers to skin it off. They rained herbicides across the West from aircraft. And, finally recognizing the role of fire, they began torching off stands of *Artemisia*. Except that in many regions there is no longer enough grass left to carry the flames from shrub to shrub. In other regions the cheatgrass turns tinder dry and burns almost every year, excluding almost everything except more cheatgrass. The one solution no one was willing to try for decades was voluntarily reducing the density of livestock, the best bunch of friends that sagebrush ever had.

In the absence of any scientific measurements from the old days, one of the best ways to judge just how much the balance of shrubs and grasses has changed out there in the Big Lonesome is to listen to what the wildlife has to tell us about it. Antelope, elk, mule deer, and bighorns all suffered severe losses around the turn of the century. In fact, antelope slipped to the brink of extinction. But it is not easy to sort out the effects of overgrazing from the toll of overhunting and, in the case of the bighorns, diseases transmitted by domestic stock. Ultimately it is some of the smaller creatures that can best reveal what has been going on among the plants underfoot.

Like the Indians before them, early settlers ate a lot of jackrabbit meat. It came from the white-tailed jackrabbit, which was then abundant and thriving in grassy openings. Now it is relatively scarce, while the less tasty black-tailed jackrabbit, which is more closely tied to sagebrush and other shrubs, is flourishing. Sharp-tailed grouse used to be fairly common in certain stretches of the high desert. But, like white-tailed jackrabbits, they preferred grasslands to scrub, and they, too, are now relatively rare here.

The curious thing is that sage grouse have declined as well—drastically. Why should a bird once so common that settlers scrambled its eggs for breakfast be disappearing, when the sagebrush that it depends upon most of the year is generally more widespread than ever?

Under grazing pressure, every 1 percent increase in sagebrush is associated with a 10 percent loss of grasses and forbs. This scenario has been played out in habitat after habitat throughout the sagebrush ecosystem, which covers one-twelfth the area of the Lower 48. Suppose the amount of sagebrush cover expands from 15 to 20 percent on a heavily used range, which typically happens. A 5 percent change; no big deal. What visitor passing by would ever notice? Except that it means that 50 percent—half!—of the grasses and forbs have been lost from the habitat. And forbs are a key to sage grouse survival through the spring and summer, especially for the chicks. Furthermore, a loss of undergrowth in prime feeding areas makes it easier for predators to see—and catch—the already vulnerable young.

Generally speaking, between 80 and 90 percent of the available forage on western public lands is allocated to livestock. Native fauna and wild horses are supposed to slug it out for the rest. Trouble is, everybody with a hoof is still after the same sprout-

The western rattlesnake (Crotalus viridis) is widespread in semiarid portions of the West, but is replaced by other species in hot deserts. Populations in northern and high-elevation parts of their range hibernate in communal dens, usually in rock crevices or caves, and often in impressive numbers. This social behavior is thought to be a response to difficult environmental conditions. The young of western rattlesnakes are born live. Upon emerging from the den in spring, young and adults alike migrate for several miles or more, usually traveling independently. Once they have gone a certain distance, they begin constantly flicking their moist tongues in and out. Scent molecules collected this way are analyzed in the snake's vomeronasal organ, located on the roof of its mouth. Where the prey density appears sufficient, the snake ceases its migration and turns to searching out individual prey using heat-sensing organs located in pits on its head. When fall arrives, the reptile retraces its route to the hibernaculum. Males often linger outside the den entrance to breed with incoming females. Both sexes may bask in the sun on warm autumn days, and their stored heat adds slightly to the den's warmth when they reenter. Presumably every extra fraction of a calorie makes the overwinter pregnancy of females that much less of a physiological burden. The result—increased production of young.

GREAT BLUE HERON, FLORIDA, JANUARY 1989

ing grass come spring. And as range scientists equate things, one cow has the same impact as two and a half elk, five deer, or fourteen antelope. Hardest hit have been the riparian, or wet meadow and streamside, areas. Although these vital habitats make up barely 2 percent of sagebrush country, they receive 50 percent of the livestock pressure.

The degradation of a riparian site is soon mirrored in the condition of wild grazers for miles around, as they also rely heavily upon streamside vegetation for both food and shelter. And in the numbers of birds, from warblers to Swainson's hawks, dependent upon water-edge trees for nesting. And in the health of wetland species such as frogs, muskrats, water shrews, waterfowl, and, of course, fish populations, which have deteriorated badly in our outback holdings over the decades.

As sagebrush habitat, riparian or otherwise, is stripped of its natural vegetative cover, it loses its ability to absorb and store water. Snowmelt and rain begin to run off more rapidly, cutting deeper channels. This drains water from the soil at greater depths. The water table as a whole drops, making conditions still more arid—more favorable to weeds, exotics, and plants armored against animal use by thorns and noxious chemicals. Competition between livestock and wildlife grows sharper. Ranchers find that their acreage won't fatten the same number of cows or sheep any longer. Struggling with lower profit margins, they call for yet more eradication of predators through poisoning programs, trapping, and shooting. . . .

A cowboy friend of mine worked ten years in Wyoming for the Animal Damage Control Branch of the U.S. Fish and Wildlife Service, which oversees predator control. He was awfully good at his job. During that time his traps and guns claimed close to four thousand coyotes, hundreds of bobcats, and scores of black bears. He destroyed hundreds more of these mammals and their offspring in dens, using everything from steel hooks and clubs to white-hot chemical bombs that burned their way through the beasts. God alone kept count of how many more this man's poisons took—including nontarget species from badgers to eagles—in the heyday of strychnine and the lethal biocide known as Compound 1080. While the use of poisons has been restricted since the early 1970s, aerial hunting efforts have been intensified to make up the difference.

According to the animals the truth about the True West is that very little remains in its original state. It has undergone some of the same process of desertification that occurred in the Near East and the Mediterranean and is going on in sub-Saharan Africa today. Such biological impoverishment has been accompanied by economic impoverishment in rangelands throughout the Big Lonesome. Put more simply, it's harder than ever to make a living off cows and sheep in the American outback, which is why so much of it holds fewer people than it did in the early decades of this century.

As our population grows ever larger and more urban our long-neglected acreage in the American outback is going to be more and more valued for its wildlife, wilderness, and recreation potential. It will be prized precisely because it is so lonesome.

The great blue heron (Ardea herodias) stands four feet tall with a six-foot wingspread. This is North America's largest representative of the Ardeidae family, which takes in the various herons, egrets, and bitterns. The spear of feathers pointing back from the head of the great blue heron is erect during displays. On the body specialized feathers form what is known as powder down. The feather ends continually disintegrate into fine absorbent particles that the bird uses to help wipe pond scum and fish oil from its other feathers. Found across most of the continent except the far North, this heron is a patient hunter that stalks in slow motion through the shallows in search of prey—or else waits in one place for the fish, frog, snake, large insect, or occasional rodent to come to it. Older, experienced individuals will gather twice the amount of food that young great blue herons can in the same amount of time. Food is swallowed whole, and undigested remains are regurgitated in pellets. Although the bird often nests in large groups, it prefers to hunt alone during the breeding period, and it will remain by itself throughout much of the year.

73

While parks, preserves, and countrysides in general become crowded and regulated to the limit, the public lands of sagebrush country will still offer a chance to really get away from it all. Which, come to think of it, is pretty much the same old elbow-room impulse that sent a lot of people riding west the first time around.

At one time or another we all dream of being cowboys or cowgirls. I don't want to see their way of life disappear. One of the things that would do the most to preserve it over the long run would be to learn how to take care of the whole sagebrush spread—an ecosystem whose vitality can be measured in terms of sage grouse, trout, and, yes, coyotes, along with native grasses and wildflowers. That is the western frontier that deserves our attention now.

I was someplace . . . way out here, way out there. I don't remember, and it really doesn't matter. I was just walking over the land. There wasn't a fence or a major landmark for days at a time. Nights at a time. It was winter and a February thaw had soaked the soil with melted snow, turning it to gumbo and mush, so I traveled part of the way under the stars and moon when the air was cold enough to set up a crust. Once in a while I would find a cairn of basalt stones piled to about man-height—the handiwork of old-time sheepherders. Built partly for navigation or as territorial markers, and partly just for something to do, they reminded me of the rock menhirs made by Eskimos in the arctic tundra, another nomad land of overwhelming openness.

Storms came and went, with more wind than sleet. I sheltered behind drifts that had snagged in thickets of big sagebrush. I boiled coffee there over small, sweet-smelling fires. Wild horses galloped by in the darkness. Residents of the New World through the Ice Age, they vanished with the last glaciers but returned in the sixteenth century, courtesy of Spanish expeditions. The escapees gathered and bred until millions roamed the American outback during the nineteenth century. They sank to a low of twenty thousand in 1970 after decades of being canned for dog food. Since passage of the Wild Horse and Burro Protection Act the following year, they have rapidly tripled their numbers. Their obvious ability to thrive in the American outback presents an interesting biopolitical quandary: Should mustangs (from the Spanish *mesteno*, meaning an unbranded feral horse) be viewed as undesirable aliens? Or is it true, as some argue, that they are reclaiming a natural niche left vacant for only a few millennia? I would somehow feel their hoofs—their weight vibrating through the half-frozen ground—and know they were coming before I actually heard them.

Antelope blurred past in a herd of about a hundred at fifty miles per hour and more. Later, staring into the firelight, I remembered the range managers' formula: One cow equals fourteen antelope. What I'd seen racing past in the moonlight was the absence of seven cows.

At dawn a small band drew near, harrying a coyote, as antelope sometimes will. They walked and trotted toward the predator in bursts until it broke and fled. Then

74

PRAIRIE FALCON, COLUMBIA PLATEAU, WASHINGTON, APRIL 1989

they came over to stand around me in a curious half-circle, edging closer and closer until one finally lost its nerve and the whole group went tearing off, the hairs of their white tailpatches fluffed out and the scent glands underneath leaving a faint aroma like sweet almonds rubbed in musk. After orbiting my morning camp once at a dead run they arced away to where the gray-green winter sagebrush met the gray February sky and reassembled to watch me a while longer. What they saw was a lone man shaking with laughter. I'm never very fast in the morning, but that antelope morning I felt hilariously slow by comparison.

Survival of the fittest begins early in life for the pronghorn. After mating, seven or eight fertilized eggs, or zygotes, begin to develop in a typical female. By about the fifth week each zygote has become an elongated mass of cell tissues known as the thread stage of the embryo. Twisting, coiling, and migrating about in the uterus, some will damage others until about a third of the embryos cease functioning and are absorbed back into the female's tissues. The remainder then attach themselves to the uterine wall, where the placentas begin to form. The embryos that attach lowest in the womb win with the richest supply of blood; they grow the most rapidly, and their expansion forces the embryos above them still farther up until they succumb for want of nourishment. In some cases the embryos—again, usually the faster-growing ones—produce a sharp projection from one end of the membrane enclosing them. Known as a necrotic tip, this point may actually spear the adjacent embryo, killing it directly. In May or June the pronghorn babies are delivered, kicking wet legs at the greened-up earth. There are usually two, occasionally triplets, often only one per doe.

After I finally got moving that morning I reached a bare ridgeline, kept clean by the wind. Upon it I built my own cairn. It was in honor of those antelope, and of all the coyotes, bobcats, eagles, storms, and mysteries of sibling rivalry in the womb that shape a pronghorn life.

On a lengthy hike you carry along with you thoughts about your job and what needs doing back home and the kind of person you are in other people's eyes . . . all the usual worries and hopes that play and replay inside our heads. But when nothing other than nature is going on outside, that baggage begins to drop off after a certain number of days. This frees up a remarkable amount of mental concentration, which then becomes focused on things like the changing murmurs of the wind and bone chips of rodents in the dried pellets of a burrowing owl. In relatively stark terrain such as the cold desert you reach the point at which a set of fresh jackrabbit tracks around the base of a bush seems a spectacle. Raven talk reverberates as if sent through a public address loudspeaker—Your attention, please!—and little dry wash gullies loom like canyons.

No judgments. No promises. No social implications. No second-guessing what everything means. It is what it is, unequivocally. Here. Now. It is a process of liberation and clarification, and I suppose it's a good part of what draws us to way-the-hell-and-gone-in-the-middle-of-nowhere places. You are not necessarily aware how

BIGHORN SHEEP, YELLOWSTONE NATIONAL PARK, WYOMING, JANUARY 1989

MALLARDS, WASHINGTON, FEBRUARY 1989

much more alert you are becoming and how thoroughly you are beginning to live in the present. Sometimes the realization doesn't come until you've reached the end of the journey, headed back toward town, and begun to lose your tuning.

Me, I came off those winter plains into Wendover, on the Utah-Nevada line, under a clean blue sky. The country was pretty close to snow-blind—solid, shimmering white except for clusters of sagebrush. Although the temperature was freezing, the day reminded me of a midsummer trip I'd made across this same route. Then the land was white from sunlight ricocheting off powdery alkali playas, with mirage fields of sagebrush floating over the ground and dust devils stinging the cracked earth with their tails.

Both times I got out of the car, walked across an enormous parking lot, opened a gilded door, and came face to face with ten thousand slot machines glowing like luminescent fish in some ocean abyss. Out of the darkness between them swam huge, pale people bearing stacks of silver coins; and fall-down gorgeous long-legged palomino-haired creatures in black panties and red velvet swallowtail dinner jackets bearing whiskey and beer and . . . what was I talking about? Oh, and I found myself grinning at overhead mirrors in smoky salons and drifting among electronically synthesized voices, bells and whistles, juke and flash, and cash registers cachunking open and shut, block-long countertops piled with food, and spinning wheels and revolving stages until I began to seriously wonder whether or not I was going to get through reentry this time.

But of course I would, before finally coming to rest at a different, cheaper hotel. And there, with a neon sign flashing outside the drawn curtains and the television next door playing through the thin walls, I'd open my backpack to find, say, a toothbrush, and all at once the odor of smoke and sagebrush would seep out. I'd sit surrounded by little bags of camping gear, wondering who that person was for whom these bags had held home, comfort, safety, even luxury; for whom this piece of twine, or that wool sock or candle had been the most precious possession in the world. That person lived lean and close to the bone. And free, the more so for his want of possessions. Lucky man, he still owns all that land out there. He can always go back where the eagles and the antelope fly, and the sagebrush horizon still seems to lead on forever.

After the spring breeding season the female mallard (Anas platyrhynchos) plucks feathers from her breast to line the nest. Just before laying the eggs, she plucks large amounts. This down will be used to cover and insulate the eggs when she leaves the nest. The plucking also creates a bare incubation patch on her breast for brooding that allows warmth to flow directly to eggs in contact with her bare skin. Male mallards remain near the incubating female for about a week, then desert her to join male flocks. During this summer period the drakes undergo a molt, replacing their bright breeding plumage with drab, mottled eclipse plumage. They also become flightless for just over a month, as do the females, when they begin their summer molt. While flight muscles grow temporarily weaker from lack of use, leg muscles build up, and so does the important layer of insulating fat. It will be needed for the coming cold weather and the long flight south to wintering grounds.

ROSEATE SPOONBILLS AND WHITE IBIS, DING DARLING NATIONAL WILDLIFE REFUGE, FLORIDA, JANUARY 1989

MUTE SWAN, BRIGANTINE
NATIONAL WILDLIFE REFUGE,
NEW JERSEY, MAY 1987

ALLIGATORS, FLORIDA, JANUARY 1989

CHAPTER FOUR

Sirens

I SEE YOU. I see you out there, torpedo shape, moving darkly at the edge of my vision. Light never seems to carry far enough in the underwater realm. Everything dissolves into the near distance, as in dreams. And, as in dreams, every other creature seems able to move quickly, while I am stuck in slow motion. What are you? Shark? A hammerhead, maybe? Leopard? Lemon? Blue? Great white?

Oh, God, I wish I weren't such a coward around sharks. Even a picture of one drains the blood from me: the mouth so ragged in a form so honed, cruising since the dawn of the world, perfect before there were animals with bones. And scientists say individual sharks may live to be hundreds of years old. You out there! Did you watch the hulls of Indian canoes and Spanish galleons pass overhead? Time honors your kind. Maybe I should as well, but I'm too frightened. I thought the water was shallow enough here to keep out the large ones. That's why I'm snorkeling around the estuary instead of farther out in this Florida bay. But here you are, anyway.

I see you! Big shadow, roving the luminous blue world without corners. Roving closer. I've got to move toward shore. Go easy. No thrashing. That only draws them. I'll swim backing in; I'm not about to turn my back on you. I mustn't feel so scared. You could sense it: smell the fear, taste a change in sea chemistry, pick up tremors in the pressure-sensitive organs along your sides, detect electrical pulses with the receptors that dot your head like pores—do all those things you are built for. And hunt harder.

You're nearer already. Closing. You, you cold-blooded. . . .

Wait! Not shark.

No! Dolphin!

No, not dolphin, either. Too rounded, somehow.

Hovering now, waiting, still incomplete in the blue mist. Are you a—what?—seal? Too huge. Sea lion? Do any visit these parts? I don't remember. I should check for others, whatever they are. Check the sides. Behind myself. Now back in front of me. Was this the front? Nothing there. Where did you go? Nothing anywhere. A school of pipefish. Mullet fry. Spokes of sunlight through a plankton cloud. . . . I see you! There! Below and rising fast. Looming straight up before me.

I'll be damned. You're a mermaid.

Mermaids is how the sailors of yore described manatees. One of the three living species inhabits the tropical west coast of Africa and the river systems leading from

During spring, amid the roaring of males defending their territories and the softer grunting of females, American alligators (Alligator mississippiensis) begin their breeding season. A pregnant female builds a nest mound four to seven feet in diameter and three feet high, in which she deposits anywhere from twenty to seventy eggs. She will then guard her nest closely against intruders over the next two and a half months. The heap of mud and rotting vegetation warms the developing eggs both by storing daytime warmth from the sun and by giving off its own heat of decomposition. Finally, hearing the peeping calls of the hatchlings as they begin to break out of the eggs, the mother alligator opens the nest to help free her offspring. The yellow coloration of the juveniles is lost as they grow older. Although they can attain a length of nearly twenty feet, they generally range from just six to twelve feet long. The crocodilian line has been around since the Jurassic period, when brontosaurs shared the swamplands. But North America's two crocodilians both nearly vanished earlier in this century as a result of uncontrolled hunting and poaching for their hides. Today an endangered population of the American crocodile (Crocodylus acutus) clings to existence in southern Florida, chiefly in the saltwater marshes of the undeveloped Cape Sable area. Alligators have rebounded rapidly in the years since they were given federal protection, but they still inhabit only a small portion of their former range, which extended from the Carolinas to Texas and eastern Mexico.

A skin diver might encounter the fish called horse-eye jacks (Caranx latus) in locales from the Indian Ocean to the Atlantic coast of North America, where they occur as far north as New Jersey. The jack family, Carangidae, takes in more than two hundred species in temperate and tropical ocean waters. Many range into estuaries and up coastal rivers, like the school of horse-eye jacks photographed here at a Florida freshwater spring. One of the better known carangids taken for food and sport is the pompano. Another, also found in the western Atlantic, is the amberjack, which grows to a length of three feet.

there toward the interior. Another swims landlocked in Amazonia. Number three ranges along the coastal areas of the Atlantic from northeastern South America to Florida. Known as the Caribbean, or West Indian, manatee, it was the mermaid described by Christopher Columbus on his New World voyage of discovery. The very first mermaid tales likely involved sightings of the manatee's Pacific counterpart, the dugong, whose various forms range from Australia to the northern end of the Red Sea. Somewhere I read that the Israelites' Ark of the Covenant, housing the tablets of moral commandments given Moses by God to guide human life, was originally covered with a dugong skin. Some early Japanese entrepreneurs used to manufacture stuffed mermaids for sale through creative work with dugong hides.

Female dugongs and manatees have distinct mammary glands located, like those of women, on their chests. They also carry their infants about in their flipper arms and cradle them at their breast for suckling. Such traits—plus maybe a seaweed wig when they surfaced in a kelp patch—might have got the mermaid legend going. But that was back in the days when beasts, humans, and their gods were a closer family, and the world was full of incantations and the likes of centaurs, minotaurs, sphinxes, and werewolves.

Upon closer inspection manatees could also be said to resemble a cross between a sausage and a waterlogged heifer. Their other early name was sea cow. The usual joke is that sailors who thought these creatures were luscious mermaids badly needed a few days in port. I think the sailors themselves were generally joking. Give them credit— a little humor counts for a lot on a wooden ship bound for the ends of the earth. But credit them, too, with finding a way to recognize our kinship with a beast that is, in the sea realm with all its strange and ancient life forms, far more like us than not.

Science passed along the old tales by classifying manatees and dugongs together in an order they named Sirenia after the half-beast, half-woman temptresses of Greek mythology. The Greeks' sirens lured sailors to their deaths on the rocks with songs no man could resist. Although manatees do chirrup and squeak somewhat like dolphins at times, they are not known to have anything like the whales' gorgeous songs. Mexicans in riverbank villages along the coast have long told quite different tales of male manatees—mermen—grunting and wriggling their way ashore on dark nights to make off with the local women.

This one is female, I think. I've only seen one live specimen before, years ago through an aquarium window. Uh-huh, definitely female. She's swimming closer still, then past me, tiny eyes set deep in a bald balloon face like buttons in an over-stuffed cushion; bristles around the mouth with its thick, muscular, cleft upper lip; obvious breasts; stout flat tail like a beaver's. Columbus was right when he noted in his journals that mermaids look a lot prettier in paintings than in person. But this is a lovely manatee. Healthy and alert. Inquisitive. More than inquisitive—friendly.

I thought manatees were supposed to be generally retiring creatures. She doesn't act wary of me at all. Now almost brushing my shoulder. Now turning slowly and

SCHOOL OF JACK FISH, CRYSTAL RIVER, FLORIDA, JANUARY 1990

MANATEE, CRYSTAL RIVER, FLORIDA, JANUARY 1990

coming back to station herself just before me. She waits, treading the water softly with a flipper. Waits, and rolls a little, presenting her side. Without knowing how I know, I am sure that she wants me to touch her. Hesitantly, feeling embarrassed, stupid, and blessed, I reach out and stroke her skin. Instead of surging away with a lash of her paddle-tail, she moves into my touch.

Who is this? What do you want from this visit? She gazes back, a half-ton of placid bulk hovering at my side. Then she lifts a flipper—there are vestigial stumps of fingernails at the end—and rolls onto her side again. Something's coming back to me. . . . Of course. I remember now: I've heard of some manatees that have grown used to the company of divers and have taken to approaching them, apparently fond of being patted or scratched. They seem to enjoy the stimulation, the grooming—the contact. I wonder who actually started it all, divers or sirens? Does it matter? A few minutes ago I was sure that a large animal was going to rise up from the sea and gouge me. Now I am fairly sure that a large sea beast has swum up to invite me to lay hands on it—to keep company. Still amazed at what it is taking in, my brain isn't working very well. That's all right. It is graceless to try to analyze a gift even as it is being given.

In 1741 Russian explorers led by Vitus Bering encountered a third member of the Sirenia. This was the sea cow, named after the party's naturalist, Georg Steller. The thing was twenty-five to thirty feet long and weighed three to four tons—a gift from the sea of elephantine proportions.

It was Bering's second expedition to chart the lands and waters between Siberia and what would become the Russian colony called Alaska. Weakened by scurvy, he captained his vessel, the *St. Peter*, onto the rocks of an island in the Commander archipelago, close to Kamchatka, at the very end of the Aleutian chain. That was where Steller's sea cows lived, perhaps fifteen hundred of them, grazing the thick kelp beds offshore in large herds. And it was where Bering died. His shipwrecked crew named the island after him and feasted on its sirens.

Overall the Sirenia look a bit like walrus, but they have altogether different origins. Walrus, along with fur seals and sea lions, are descendants of a primitive, bearish carnivore that returned to the sea. True seals arose from an otterlike ancestor. Sperm whales, orcas, and dolphins—the toothed cetaceans—are thought to come from a piglike progenitor. Something more on the order of an anteater spawned the great baleen whales. During the Eocene, the earliest epoch after the dinosaurs' demise, yet another type of mammal gave rise to three lines of creatures currently grouped together as the subungulates: hyraxes, anomalous little African beasts that resemble hoofed rodents with tusks; elephants; and sirens, the only vegetarians among truly aquatic mammals. Elephants and sirens still share an unusual tooth succession pattern in which new grinding molars replace old ones by growing in from the back of the jawbone and moving toward the front. Cow elephants also have mammary glands between their front legs that take on a shape very much like human breasts when the elephant is pregnant or nursing.

One of the three surviving manatee species, the West Indian manatee (Trichechus manatus) inhabits the west coast of the Americas in warm latitudes. During colonial times its U.S. range took in estuaries and coastal streams from the Carolinas to Texas. The present population, numbering less than a thousand, is concentrated in southern Florida's waters. The peaceable, four-hundred- to twelve-hundred-pound creature is protected from the sort of commercial hunting for its hide, oil, and meat—marketed as "sea beef"—that decimated its numbers earlier. But it is increasingly at risk from the propellers of speeding motorboats, and from urban developments that invade ever more of its critical shoreline habitat. A close relative used to live in the icy Bering Sea between the tip of the Aleutian chain and Kamchatka. It was twenty-five feet long or more and weighed several tons. This was the Steller's sea cow. Discovered in 1741, it was extinct by 1769, every last one having been taken for meat by fur hunters on their way to raid seal colonies. Though a placid grazer, the manatee is anything but slow-witted. It displays a good deal of curiosity and social interaction, often joining with others of its kind in bouts of mutual nuzzling and grooming, speaking in a language of high squeals and chirrups. Captive manatees have proven able to learn rapidly and remember what they have learned for at least a year. The sirens' closest living relative happens to be the elephant. The two lines arose from a common ancestor some fifty million years ago.

87

PURPLE GALLINULE, FLORIDA, JANUARY 1989

Traditionally, the Sirenia were not credited with a great deal of intelligence, in part simply because they are slow, generally easygoing munchers of submarine pastures. Yet Steller noticed that after one of the giant sea cows was harpooned, others in its group would circle the victim, apparently trying to provide aid or comfort. Sometimes they would shove against the harpooner's rowboat. One male swam back and forth for two days close to its mate, which lay dead on the beach.

Upon closer study all the Sirenia have proven to be highly sociable beasts, playful and solicitous of one another, with a well-developed sense of curiosity. Not surprisingly, tests with captive manatees reveal a good capacity for learning, coupled with the ability to remember lessons for at least one year. What kind of knowledge was stored in Steller's sea cow? Did this species inhabit any other parts of the Aleutian chain or was it an isolated population? No one can say. Twenty-seven years after its discovery, the greatest of the sirens was gone, liquidated for meat by the seal fur hunters who had arrived to plunder the northern frontier Bering helped open. That is one of the very few hard facts about the species ever gathered. We don't even have enough tatters of information to re-create its existence in our minds in a meaningful way. In other words, this life form can't even feed our thoughts anymore. It is extinct as a source of ideas.

The breasts of my mermaid friend are well enough developed that I wonder at first if she has a nursing young one with her. It appears not. Perhaps she had one and recently lost it. To sharks, possibly. Or to other ancient life forms: the American crocodile still dwells in the salt marshes at Florida's southernmost tip—its last refuge. With specimens longer than twenty feet reported, what's left of this species still qualifies as a formidable predator. The more common alligator prefers freshwater swamps. Since manatees—more so than dugongs—move readily between saltwater and freshwater habitats inland, they must deal with Florida's alligators now and then as well.

Freshwater is where I think my acquaintance is heading. She keeps swimming a few yards toward shore in the direction of the river's mouth, then pauses to look back my way, waits until I catch up, and strokes on. It isn't far to the mangrove shallows, where crabs sidle toward shelter among the roots as our shadows fall upon them. I can touch bottom here, kicking up clouds of root-trapped silt with my rubber imitations of a flipper. My facemask gives me a periscope view of wood ibises flapping toward shoreline trees. Roseate spoonbills wade the tide flats, sieving small fish, shrimp, and the tiniest of the crabs, swinging their paddle-bills through the water, shimmering hot pink reflections across the drab flats.

Closer by, brown pelicans are diving on a school of fish. I'd like to swim over among them and try to see them catch their meals underwater. (They flare open the huge lower bill pouch that everyone used to think was just for storing fish, and the sudden expansion vacuums in nearby prey.) But I might lose contact with the siren. I don't want to miss wherever it is that she seems intent upon leading me. She may look slow, but she isn't all that easy to keep up with.

Long toes that distribute weight make it easy to walk across lily pads as well as soft mud for the purple gallinule (Porphyrula martinica). Found from the southeastern United States to northern Argentina, these marsh dwellers are sometimes as noisy as they are boldly colored. They seem especially conspicuous when compared to other members of the generally quite secretive rail family, Rallidae. Although the biology of the purple gallinule is still poorly understood, it appears that the birds live in social groups consisting of four to five related animals, sometimes as many as eight. Six to eight eggs are usually laid in floating nests built of heaped, hollow-stemmed vegetation. Nonbreeders in the group assist the parents in defending the nesting territory and feeding the developing young. Not long after the eggs hatch, the brood is moved to a nearby nest, possibly to avoid parasite buildup or predators. Purple gallinules forage on a number of different aquatic plants. They take aquatic insects as well, along with crustaceans, snails, and frogs. From time to time they prey upon the eggs and young of other birds, including the northern jacana, a lily-walker from an unrelated avian family. During late summer and fall the gallinules turn to the ripening seeds of wild rice.

Of North America's seven grebe species the pied-billed grebe (Podilymbus podiceps) has the widest geographic range and the most solitary habits. It also tends to use freshwater lakes and ponds throughout the year, whereas many populations of larger grebes move from inland breeding areas to wintering grounds along the seacoast. In the southern part of their range pied-billed grebes may nest year-round. The young often ride on a parent's back as it swims, and when it dives, they may go along as well, hanging onto the adult's feathers with their bills. Grebes regularly eat large quantities of their own feathers. Half the stomach contents of a pied-billed grebe may consist of its own plumage. Newborn chicks without well-developed feathers will eat those of their parents. Scientists are not certain what this is all about, but reason that the feathers help pad the stomach against the needle-sharp tips of fishbones to prevent puncturing. Feather balls also slow digestion so that the stomach acids have time to dissolve bones before they pass on to the intestinal tract. Grebes represent a very ancient avian line that was swimming in this continent's lakes while dinosaurs roamed the shores, and the gizzards of these birds never developed the kind of advanced musculature needed to crush bones before they reach the stomach.

Adult manatees weigh anywhere from four hundred to twelve hundred pounds, occasionally more, and may be from seven feet long to twice that length. Adapted to tropical and subtropical waters, they wear no insulating layer of blubber beneath their skin, but do store a fair amount of fat and oil in their flesh. Unusually thick, heavy bones probably act somewhat like diving weights, making it easier for them to keep their buoyant bodies submerged at comfortable depths. The effectiveness of bones in transmitting sound vibrations may help explain the manatee's excellent sense of hearing. By contrast, its eyesight appears limited—out of water, anyway.

I don't notice my companion paying much attention to movements when she lifts her head above the surface as we proceed upstream. But she reacts to many sounds before I do. Strangely she does not always seem to pick up the noise of motorboats right away. Once she does she sinks toward the bottom until they pass. She can stay down without breathing for upwards of a quarter of an hour. I have to swim for the side of the river until the craft speed by.

Now and then she snatches a bite of plants from the bottom, working them into her mouth with her fleshy upper lip. She also feeds on floating vegetation. The average manatee consumes something like one hundred pounds or more of forage daily, or roughly one-tenth of its body weight. My siren seems familiar with the river's course, and at two or three places undulates over to a bank lined with grass and pops up to graze there while treading water with her tail. Each time there is a burst of surprised frogs over her head.

Somewhere along this watershed, and in streams and ponds throughout the Southeast, dwells another type of amphibian: salamanders that happen to be known as sirens. Whereas typical salamanders leave the water to take up life on land once they mature, these adult sirens retain both the larval form's aquatic mode of existence and its feathery gills. As in manatees, the process of specializing for life as a swimmer has resulted in their forelegs being reduced in size and their hind limbs being lost altogether. These hydrodynamic amphibians look as much like eels as salamanders. Yard-long eels, in the case of the greater siren, found from Delaware to northern Mexico.

The tropics and subtropics seem so generous to life forms conceived in earlier ages mainly because they are such stable environments compared to the temperate regions. I'm thinking of my homeland to the north, where everything had to start fresh after the glaciers scraped away the old order—sending the elders into retirement in the Sun Belt—and where the ice ages commence all over again in miniature with the onset of each winter.

Sharks, frogs, salamanders, crocs, gators, alligator snapping turtles, coral snakes, armadillos, opossums, manatees. . . . To the list of old-timers I add the anhingas perched on a snag mired in a midriver sandbar as we pass. Called snakebirds, they lack the oil glands and tightly knit fine feather structure that waterproof modern birds. Thus they float with their bodies practically submerged, while their serpentine heads dart back and forth above. After a session of diving through the water trying to

PIED-BILLED GREBE, EVERGLADES NATIONAL PARK, FLORIDA, JANUARY 1989

impale fish, they perch with their wings held open to the sun. While this helps dry their feathers, making flight somewhat easier, the main purpose of such a posture is now thought to be thermoregulation: it lets the snakebird, which has an unusually low metabolic rate, absorb more warmth from the sun.

Not far past the anhingas, I haul out to rest for a moment on a silty bank tracked by racoons. It was tough enough to match the siren's pace in the open water of the bay; against the river current, lazy as it is here, the journey has become a struggle. She still checks on me every so often and lingers while I catch up, but I believe her interest in our encounter has worn thin, and she would just as soon continue upriver on her own. Maybe not. She has turned and is rippling my way, her broad back just breaking the surface. I'll go, but I don't know for how long. My thigh muscles hurt from powering the flippers, and my waterlogged fingers are beginning to look like manatee skin.

Just as I decide the next bend in the river will be my last, she turns into a narrow tributary. It looks like an alligator-size channel to me—the kind where you sometimes find rows of dragons snoozing on each bank in the heat. But I take it. Instantly the water clears and brightens. I feel as though I were swimming in an aquarium. No dragons ashore. Only more long-necked swamp birds—herons and egrets—and a white-tailed deer. Within a hundred yards the channel ends in a crystalline pool where the spring that feeds it wells up. There must be a dozen manatees waiting. I halfway expect them to celebrate our arrival. But just two come over to greet my siren, saying something in high-pitched manatee voices. Only one of them continues on to inspect me, and only with a passing glance. Then it moves back to the end of the pool. Far better to be ignored, I tell myself, than to disrupt their afternoon. I settle in to watch.

This being late May, the herd includes two fairly new babies. Both sexes of manatees care for the young, and I notice a male cradling one sixty-pound infant the same way a mother would. He takes it up for air every minute or so, while a female, probably the mother herself, crops water lilies close by. There is some nuzzling and manatee talk among the group, and I notice one using its flipper to scratch my siren on her side, just about where I first did. One has strings of spirogyra—the filamentous green algae sometimes called mermaid's tresses—snagged on a flipper. Another has streaks of algae actually growing on its sunlit back. The most noticeable detail about this group is the patterns of white lines on nearly all their backs; stripes for some, a dense hatchwork for others. They are scars from boat propellers.

Both dugongs and manatees have been hunted so heavily for the rich, fatty, red meat underneath the hide that most siren species today are in danger of following Steller's sea cow into extinction. In the heyday of conquistadors and converts, the Caribbean manatee's meat was doubly prized. Since it came from a "fish," it could be eaten on Catholic fast days when mammal meat was off-limits. A brief, bloody U.S. trade in "sea beef" in the latter part of the nineteenth century sliced away the manatee's U.S. range along the Gulf of Mexico and eastern seaboard until only Florida was

FLORIDA PANTHER, FLORIDA, JANUARY 1989

AMERICAN FLAMINGOS, GULF OF MEXICO, NOVEMBER 1987

left, with an occasional siren seen northward along the coast of Georgia and the Carolinas during summer.

Today, with hunting banned and poaching minimal, Florida's remnant manatee population, estimated at a thousand or less, is still declining. A single, simple thought could reverse this trend: Slow down your boat a little along channels frequented by the beasts. Many folks have proved willing. For others giving up a speed thrill just to keep from running over some sea cow is apparently asking too much.

And so the last of the U.S. manatees continue to suffer the death of a thousand cuts. Or are rammed at full throttle. Those die more quickly. For all the eons that went into siren-shaping to be brought to a close this way. . . . I don't want to think about it now. Instead I take hold of a root at the pool's edge and float absolutely motionless, resting and continuing to absorb the spectacle of mermaid society. It is one of the most peaceable places I have ever been. After some time—I couldn't begin to guess how much—I become aware of the sound of a hard wind. I don't pay much attention until it strikes me that I've no business being able to hear wind underwater. As I come up to look around at the sky, my head suddenly feels cold. Something is wrong. Wrong with this whole situation. The cold intensifies, causing me to shiver. The manatees' heads are all out of the water, staring straight at me. I'm shivering uncontrollably now. . . .

Then I awake in a blizzard back in the mountains. I lie slumped against the wall on a bench inside a drafty shack—an ice fishing shack in the middle of a frozen lake. Somewhere underneath my feet are lake trout, whitefish, pike. Some frogs burrowed into the bottom muck, waiting for spring. And crayfish—crawdads too cold to crawl. I peer out the plastic-sheet window a long time, watching the snow stream by sideways. For a while I hold on to that warm, fuzzed feeling close enough to the dream that I still hope I might slide back into it. Dreams never work that way, though, even if you do make it back to sleep.

A gust of wind makes the shack squeak and drives spindrift through the cracks. It occurs to me that my subsconscious has been trying hard to point out that I could be spending this January day more wisely, or at least more warmly. My bladder is also sending important messages. Sooner or later I am going to have to shuffle out past the canvas flap that serves as a door and into that bitter wind. I won't stay sleepy too long out there. I will remember the dream, though.

At one time it was hoped that manatees could be used to keep open waterways from becoming choked by water hyacinth, an aggressive invader from Africa. But while the hyacinth has continued to spread, manatee numbers have only continued to shrink. The sirens could still be used as a nontoxic form of weed control one day, if they can recover. It has also been pointed out that a flourishing manatee population could support a managed offtake of sea beef for the market, benefiting the local economy. For that matter, sirens might play a pivotal role in complex aquaculture schemes of the future. And who knows what manatees might ultimately reveal to re-

A common display of greater flamingos (Phoenicopterus ruber) involves stylized stretching with waving of the head and rapid opening and closing of the wings. The dance called the flamenco was named for this bird. The Spanish named the bird after the rosy-complexioned peoples of northern France and Belgium—los Flamingos, the Flemings. Flamingos take their vivid color from the carotene pigments of the shrimp and other crustaceans they feed upon. Flamingos are filter-feeders. Comblike projections from the mandibles strain food from seawater as the bird swishes its beak back and forth through the water. Or the bird can hold its head steady while the tongue acts as a pump, sucking water in through the strainers and expelling it, repeating this cycle up to four times a second. The flamingo feeds with its head upside down so that the upper half of the beak is lowest in the water. Most of the population along the Florida coast today is considered semidomestic, as it arose from escaped captive birds. But wild flamingos do pay an occasional visit. The species breeds in the West Indies, Yucatán, and as far south as the Galapagos Islands.

95

Half the height of a great blue heron, the little blue heron (Egretta caerulea), of the southeastern United States and Mexico, is at home in both freshwater and saltwater marshes. Fish are the staple of this bird's diet, and it takes slightly larger ones than do the other waders in its size range. Alone, it hunts in typical heron-style, slowly stalking the shallows and watching for prey. But it has greater success when it follows other species, such as the similar-size white ibis, which stirs up the bottom as it probes the muck with its bill. Simply by walking from one spot to the next, the ibis inadvertently flushes prey for the heron trailing two or three feet behind it. Little blue herons nest in colonies that include nonbreeding birds. Since unmated males will approach females left alone on the nest, the breeding males seldom depart for more than a few minutes at a time, and basically go without feeding until the last of the two to five eggs is laid.

searchers in the fields of psychology, medicine, and so forth. After all, the armadillo, so antique and armored and generally ignored, turned out to be crucial to work on a cure for leprosy. Shark physiology, meanwhile, is being examined for clues about how to stave off old age; the extremely high level of urea found in the bloodstream of these long-lived beasts may somehow slow down the process of aging in cells.

But why should we always have to trot out arguments suggesting that a creature might pay its way as a crop or that it possibly holds the cure for cancer? It ought to be reward enough simply to know that the animal is out there somewhere, exercising its own right to exist.

To know that things are where they belong, doing what they are supposed to do, is immensely satisfying in its own right. And it provides hope that the living world is operating as it should for the long-term survival of the human species as well. Conservation is not, ultimately, about saving this species or that one. It is about saving the process, power, and mystery of creation.

The belief that every creature has the fundamental right to exist is implicit in our endangered species laws. These mandate that we try very hard to keep a species that is already very scarce from vanishing altogether. They make no guarantees that once the creature is safe from extinction we will work to make it abundant. Yet shouldn't every creature also have a right to fullness; that is, not merely to exist, but to exist in sufficient numbers over a sufficiently large portion of its natural range that it can produce variations, compete, and continue to evolve along the lines of its original potential? In our species we call this the right to life, liberty, and the pursuit of happiness. Animal species that lack such a dynamic role are ecologically crippled, even if we manage to salvage a few. They become relics tucked away in a few last refuges like museum pieces.

Obviously such a fate is better than oblivion. However, any species kept holed up too long with too few members is likely to turn genetically and behaviorally brittle—ingrown—and, thus, to turn into something else. It is the essence of every living thing that it is ceaselessly *becoming*, however dramatic or slight the increments of change. Our choice is to shift beyond talk of merely saving species to giving each one room to manifest itself in robust populations. Turn it loose to interact with other big, vigorous, wild populations as nature intended, and see what it can show us. See what we can become together.

One of the most rewarding things of all about each animal's existence may be the unique way in which it adds to the range and texture of the world inside our heads. The human mind evolved in an animal landscape, and the way in which our imagination works is one of the results of this process. We had to be adept at envisioning animals in order to survive both as hunters and as the hunted. We had good cause to fear the dark; good cause to sing with joy at the sight of a ripe plain filled with fellow beasts. We needed to be able to build plans in our heads for the catching and more plans to avoid being caught. Where would the animal I have in mind be feeding? Hiding? Stalking? What is it most interested in this time of day? This time of year?

LITTLE BLUE HERON IN MANGROVE ROOTS, DING DARLING NATIONAL WILDLIFE REFUGE, FLORIDA, JANUARY 1989

SNOWY EGRET, BRIGANTINE NATIONAL WILDLIFE REFUGE, NEW JERSEY, MAY 1989

Which way will it come? What would it do if it sees me acting this way? Making this sound? Will it act the same if it has its young along? If I have mine with me?

Our imagination remains a natural habitat for the beasts around us, even for those we have encountered only through words or film. They stimulate our creativity by their ability to wander at will through our innermost realm, whence spring curiosity, visions, and the seeds of new ideas. They gave us dreams. They give us dreams still.

That's what good a manatee is.

No, I've never gone swimming with a wild manatee; never even seen one, just as most people who care about whales or musk-oxen have never laid eyes on the animals themselves. Not yet. Our dreams of doing so—and our pleasure in knowing that some are still out there waiting in the meanwhile—are a resource that must be guarded as carefully as something so precious deserves. For it has to do ultimately with the nature of the soul.

We change so much of the world, and yet we understand so little. Does anyone know what a soul really is? Do we alone possess one? What about the gorilla that makes jokes in sign language? The mother grizzly that spends a summer afternoon repeatedly sliding down a cool snowbank with her cub on her lap? The coyote that growls and runs in its sleep, dreaming coyote dreams? The manatee seeking the human swimmer for company? Could it be that the soul abides neither in humans nor in any other things, but in the connections between them?

I don't know. But I believe that someday I will swim with manatees. Someday I will scratch one's itch and make us both glad.

Snowy egrets (Egretta thula) are some of the most active feeders among egrets and their close allies, the herons, and they may have the most varied foraging techniques. In addition to running down prey—fish, amphibians, crustaceans, and insects—they purposefully stir the bottom muck with their feet to drive out animals. They also follow other wading species, especially the glossy ibis, to catch creatures roiled up by the leading bird's feet. Being probers, which sense their food by touch, ibises are less aware of what is swimming or floating around them than the egrets are. Finally, snowy egrets practice the more common heron and egret behavior of standing in one spot motionless as a branch of driftwood, then striking snake-quick with their long dagger of a beak as prey comes within range.

99

SANDHILL CRANES, NEW MEXICO, FEBRUARY 1987

RED FOX, MOUNT MCKINLEY NATIONAL PARK, ALASKA, MARCH 1988

WILD TURKEY, NEW MEXICO, NOVEMBER 1989

CHAPTER FIVE
Los Guajalotes

IGNACIO IS THE *VAQUERO*, OR COWBOY, for Rancho Pallan, which is in the north central Mexican state of Chihuahua and encompasses twenty-two thousand acres of the Sierra Madre at elevations between roughly seventy-five hundred and nine thousand feet. He and his wife are usually the only people on the place. There was a baby, but the baby died. Ignacio, who is of mixed Indian and Spanish blood, goes by the nickname Nacho. I don't know his wife's name. It is not a very good idea to ask Nacho questions about his woman. The Sierra Madre is hard country, and women are scarce.

In his muleback circuits of the rangeland, where tall grasses and agaves grow beneath open forests of oak, pine, and juniper, this *vaquero* does what is expected. He tends to the cattle. He mends fence lines. He warns off trespassers and poachers and kills coyotes and pumas. A mountain lion rug lies in every room of the main house. Skins of seven more big cats and one cub hang from a wire in the storage shed.

Nacho also shoots animals to eat or, ammunition being expensive, kills them with hurled stones. Sometimes during his rounds he discovers caves or ruins of pre-Columbian Indian houses and explores them. He finds paintings, carved figures, stone grinding bowls, and pieces of weapons and pottery. Once in a dry wash near the top of the land he found three gold Spanish coins of conquistador vintage. Maybe a Spaniard lost the coins there through bad luck of one degree or another. More likely an Apache did, after raiding them from a valley town. The possibilities of more gold among the mesas are tantalizing, but probably empty. For us the most important thing about Nacho was that he knew where to find something else we wanted.

We from the outside—a team from the U.S. Army, another from the Mexican federal government, myself, and a couple of other gringo volunteers—wanted to track down and capture *los guajalotes*. That translates as "turkeys": wild Mexican turkeys, which have become rare. We had a plan to help make them less so. What we were after was two or three pickup truckfuls of the big, gallinaceous birds with snoods, wattles, caruncles, and white-tipped tailfeathers, both fertile hens and lusty toms. This turkey-trapping project had been years in the making as paperwork shuffled back and forth between the United States and Mexico. Once fieldwork was finally approved further bureaucratic delays combined with unseasonal storms to wreck

*Largest by far of the gallinaceous, or fowllike, birds on the continent, the turkey (*Meleagris gallopavo*) comes in five (some say six) subspecies. The most common is* sylvestris, *native to eastern woodlands. This is the bird whose meat helped sustain the Pilgrims and later settlers, and the one Benjamin Franklin proposed as the symbol of the United States. It lost to the bald eagle by a single vote in Congress. The subspecies* merriami, *of the West, can be told by the amount of white coloring on its wings. Then there is* mexicana, *commonly called the Mexican wild turkey, or Gould's turkey. Distinguished by white-tipped tailfeathers, it is found only in the mountains of southernmost Arizona and New Mexico, along with portions of the Sierra Madre in northern Mexico. This continent's wild turkeys underwent drastic declines due to loss of habitat to agriculture, overgrazing by livestock, diseases transmitted by domestic fowl, and market hunting at roosts. Management programs have reintroduced the birds to much of their former range. But* mexicana, *the ancestor of all Thanksgiving turkeys, is endangered both in Mexico and the United States.*

No owl in the world is smaller than the sparrow-size elf owl (Micrathene whitneyi), whose loud, cackling call seems to come from a bigger bird. Native to the American Southwest and Mexico, it is a common resident of landscapes bristling with saguaro and other large cacti, of riparian desert habitat shaded by sycamore trees, and of the oak forests found at higher elevations within the Sonoran region. Males arrive on breeding grounds before females to select nest sites. These are very often the abandoned nest cavities of gila woodpeckers and flickers. Holes in the fleshy saguaro, cardon, and organ pipe cacti offer shade and relatively cool temperatures during the day. Then the solar energy absorbed and stored by the cactus mass provides a bit of extra warmth through the cold desert night. Males compete for such prime lodging not only with other elf owls but also with a number of different types of native birds. The male feeds the female from the beginning of courtship until the young in the nest are halfway to fledging. As a rule this little nocturnal hunter concentrates on insects, sometimes hovering by blossoms to scare the bugs feeding there into flight so that it can snatch them with its beak. It may also bring back an occasional lizard or small snake.

three expeditions in a row. Now time and money were both running short. Worse, the flocks were about to break up for the spring mating period. Even if we could still catch hens a few at a time, our bait would cease to lure toms. The males essentially lose their appetite for anything except gobbling, strutting, fighting, and copulating. And we didn't want to disturb either sex during the breeding season, anyway. There are too few new babies born to this line of wild fowl as it is.

So, toward the end of March, we made our way through the mountains to Rancho Pallan, banging along a dirt track in a heavy pickup truck, and Nacho led us straight to the last feeding site of a huge, mixed flock of males and females with their young. We set our traps and began spreading bait around them. No sooner had we baited the last one than a wolf wind out of the west brought in a blizzard that stopped us cold. The unseasonal storm was a lovely one, engraving the high landscape in black and white. In respect to the work at hand, though, it was a sort of natural disaster.

The Sierra Madre Occidental officially ends near the international boundary, some ninety miles north of Rancho Pallan. Yet the unravelings of this great plaited mass of high country extend well into southeastern Arizona and the adjoining edge of New Mexico. Here the Mule, Whetstone, Dragoon, Huachuca, and Chiricahua mountains carry much the same history of gold, Spaniards, and Apache raids.

During the 1870s the U.S. Army built a special outpost among the Huachuca Mountains as part of its effort to quell the brilliant guerilla campaign led by the Apache Geronimo. Afterward Fort Huachuca was phased out of commission, but it was later revitalized and today serves as the Army's global communications command headquarters, its principal electronics proving ground, and a key intelligence center and school. The post's seventy-three thousand acres also comprise quite a bit of prime wildlife habitat.

Like the northern Sierra Madre, the Huachucas rise from a high, grassy Sonoran plain spiked by cholla cactus and mesquite, up through oak and juniper and then pine woodlands alive with clear streams, and on to cool peaks capped by winter snows and summer wildflowers. Climbing the slope from bottom to top is the ecological equivalent of traveling from the subtropics nearly to the subarctic. Within this compression of life zones dwells an array of mammals that includes ringtails and coati, two little-known members of the racoon family; Coues white-tailed deer, a subspecies unique to the Southwest; pronghorn antelope; and black bears. There have been incidents of ringtails chewing wires in super-secret satellite data processing rooms, rattlesnakes coiled up under control consoles, deer occupying the tank gunnery range, and javelinas overrunning the vehicle compound.

The Huachucas also harbor a spectrum of feathered animals that draws birders from across the United States. Among the 315 or so species that a serious lister could tally here are the parrotlike fruit-eaters called elegant trogons and fifteen different kinds of hummingbirds. Plus wild turkeys. Unfortunately they are the wrong kind of turkeys. They are Merriam's turkeys, *Meleagris gallopavo merriami*, which originally

ELF OWL IN SAGUARO CACTUS, SONORAN DESERT, ARIZONA, JULY 1984

SCRUB JAY, MONTEREY, CALIFORNIA, SEPTEMBER 1989

lived farther north. The right kind, native to the mountains of southern Arizona and New Mexico as well as the northern Sierra Madre, is *Meleagris gallopavo mexicana*, the Mexican wild turkey, also known as Gould's turkey. At the moment it is endangered on the U.S. side, reduced by past overhunting and overgrazing to several tiny, isolated bands. For the same old reasons—too many people, guns, cows, and sheep—it is rapidly disappearing from its last strongholds in Old Mexico as well.

U.S. military bases are on public land and, therefore, subject to the same basic natural resource protection laws that apply, for example, to national forests. The public is not widely aware of this, nor of the fact that portions of many bases are open for wildlife viewing and other forms of public recreation. Several posts have what amount to exemplary environmental programs. The reason we were at Rancho Pallan following Nacho around is that wildlife biologists employed by the Army had devised a scheme to take turkeys from the Sierra Madre in order to establish a breeding *mexicana* population at Fort Huachuca, thereby restoring a native U.S. life form. The Mexican biologists involved in the project were to transplant one or two flocks of the captured birds to an outlying mountain range in Chihuahua, thereby establishing some alternate breeding populations that would help ensure the future of the subspecies as a whole.

At Rancho Pallan the snow finally eased off, and the next day's sun began to melt the open spots. Nacho ran down the tracks and scratchings of another good-size flock on the side hills of a sandy wash. Close by where the ravine opened onto a level stretch, we once more spread our corn bait and set up our drop net. It was a large affair that we pitched like a circus tent on poles. When the moment of truth arrived, an explosive charge would break the fastenings and send the tent sliding down the poles to land on top of the birds and bait. Elsewhere we had another crew tending miniature cannons that would shoot a net out over any *guajalotes* coming in to peck corn, and in yet another place we had a series of simple box traps. Now it was only a matter of waiting.

Turkeys have a reputation for being remarkably dumb. The reputation is undeserved. Domestic turkeys may have had the brains largely bred out of them, along with their normal survival instincts, but wild turkeys are wary, hardy, and resourceful. In all they are canny enough that sportsmen throughout the United States rank them as one of their favorite quarries. In other words, these folks are not ashamed to say that they have spent the day matching wits with turkeys. Once you've watched the iridescent birds treading across a forest floor, coruscating in the dappled light, recording every whisper and twist of a leaf in the tilt of their heads, you can better appreciate why.

One of the other gringo volunteers had two overriding interests in his life: hunting wild turkeys, which he did almost continuously, following the spring and fall game season from state to state; and conserving wild turkeys, which was why he was here. He owned a collection of more than two hundred different turkey calls made of

Scrub jays (Aphelocoma coerulescens) occupy much of the West, choosing the sort of brushy habitat described by their name. They are absent from the Midwest and the East, yet a small, threatened subspecies inhabits southern Florida. Typical scrub jays take insects in the warm months, then turn to ripening berries and nuts, much like their close relative the piñon jay (Gymnorhinus cyanocephalus). Scrub jays cache their seeds and nuts in various hiding places, sometimes after raiding the caches of acorn woodpeckers. Like squirrels, the birds are important dispersers of the plants whose seeds they gather, as they drop food en route and also leave more than they consume scattered around in caches. Like other members of the crow, or corvid, family, scrub jays have been seen riding on the bodies of deer and other ungulates, picking off ticks and flies. Also like most corvids, scrub jays raid the nests of other birds for eggs and nestlings. At the same time they themselves suffer more nest failures as a result of predation than from any other cause, at least in the Florida subspecies. Perhaps this is why nesting pairs there are often accompanied by helpers—nonbreeding members of the flock—that assist in defense, lowering the rate of nest loss to predators. Jays actively mob enemies, swarming around them en masse with raucous cries.

everything from hollow legbones to stone friction pads to rubber diaphragms. He had brought along about two dozen. He tried them all in the hope of enticing some toms our way. At one point I glimpsed two males squaring off in a dominance display, each one suddenly erupting in spread pinions and quivering violently with every feather stretched tautly on end. If there had been a live electric cable anywhere in this country, I would have thought the animals had just stepped on it. Then they glimpsed us, and vanished. We sweetened the trap with a bit more corn, and settled in to wait again. Then we waited some more, checking each morning and evening for fresh signs of use, finding little. Little or nothing.

Our waiting seemed part of a greater stillness suspended in the thin air and hard light arcing over this highland. We watched piñon jays float from branch to branch of the Apache pines and shake snowdrops loose to flare in the sun. We walked behind Nacho toward the very top of the range to see some ancient cliff dwellings and sat on the time-worn ledges in the afternoon rays, watching golden eagles hunt the ridgelines. We talked about ivory-billed woodpeckers, believed extinct until a recent dispatch from Cuba offered hope that a few pairs remain on earth after all; why couldn't some be here in this massive swell of backcountry, where survivors were reported in decades past?

Finding ourselves with more and more days to fill with something besides silence and expectation, we talked about many things. We talked about the agaves growing around us with their bayonet leaves and towering flower spikes; about how the pulpy basal stem of the plant is the source of true mescal liquor. The other volunteer gringo happened to be an expert on the moths whose larvae feed on the agave's basal tissues; these are the "worms" placed in mescal bottles to show that you are getting the genuine stuff. Wild agave has been brewed into strong drink since prehistory, and some varieties have been cultivated for either booze or sisal fiber since at least the days of the Aztec empire. By now hundreds of different agaves have been classified, and it appears that, for almost every one, a different species of agave moth exists to pollinate it. Many more remain to be identified, even while some are disappearing as settlement transforms ever more of the canyons and mesas. In his wanderings through remote Mexican territory to collect new forms, the moth gringo had come upon dead people every so often, killed for reasons as nameless and unremarked as the corpses themselves. Maybe some of them just got too drunk on mescal to stay out of death's way.

Creeping along on our bellies through the grasses to check one trap site at dawn, a Mexican biologist and I heard a long howl issue from the valley on the other side of a knoll. It had a strange, deep resonance to it, and once the last echo had died away, the quiet felt stronger than before. *El coyote?* I asked. *No señor, es el lobo.* It was one of the world's last Mexican wolves, another subspecies once common in the American Southwest. At the moment it does not look as though it is going to be able to stay out of the way of extinction.

As we sat around the ranch house one restless afternoon beneath the animal skulls

MULE DEER, POINT LOBOS, CALIFORNIA, SEPTEMBER 1989

and hides that hung from every wall, Nacho developed a bad headache. I asked what he supposed the cause was, thinking that I might have something in my medical kit that would help. He frowned impatiently and said the cause was an evil spirit sent his way by a witch, as if any fool could have diagnosed that. If I cut his hair, he added, the pain might leave. I cut it, and he improved. Then he passed along to me rumors that a few Mexican grizzlies were still holed up thereabouts where *el lobo* still howls despite the use of poisoned bait by ranchers. Nacho said: "A *vaquero* on another ranch, he saw *el oso plateado*. *Sí*, the silvery bear. He has killed many black bears, this man; he would surely know the difference. Also a logger told a friend of mine he saw tracks—tracks that could only have been from *el oso plateado*; there is no mistaking the long claws."

I would soon be on my way to search for silver-tipped bears in the next mountain range to the east in Chihuahua, the Sierra del Nido. There, grizzlies were seen in 1964 and again in 1967. Definitely seen—and definitely killed. No one has made a positive identification of any since. (Nor did I come up with anything other than big droppings, which were very likely from one of the black bears that grow to impressive sizes there on a diet rich in acorns, pine nuts, and manzanita and juniper berries.) But jaguars still pass through every so often. They even make rare forays into Arizona and Texas, though, again, it gets hard to separate fact from possible spoor, and spoor from sheer speculation, like legends of old gold and lost lives.

I began to feel as if we were all sitting around telling each other ghost stories. A live turkey or two might shake us out of the dream. We moved our trap site and started waiting all over again in the stillness.

Wild turkeys average seventeen pounds for toms, half as much for hens, and they spend most of their time on the ground foraging for berries, acorns and other nuts and seeds, insects, and, to a lesser extent, sprouting grasses and leaf buds. They can't fly far at all before tiring. They seldom fly, anyway, except to escape danger and to avoid predators in general by roosting each night in groups on the branches of trees. They would rather hike uphill, feeding as they go, and then glide down to a roost than flap up to reach one. Such limited mobility may partially explain how turkey populations could have become isolated enough from one another to begin evolving as more or less distinct subspecies.

Most authorities recognize five subspecies of *Meleagris gallopavo*, all exclusively North American birds. The most familiar by far is *Meleagris gallopavo sylvestris*, the turkey of the continent's eastern deciduous woodlands. This is the bird usually depicted in one hand of a Pilgrim forefather while the other hand holds a blunderbuss. It is also the bird that Benjamin Franklin proposed as the U.S. national symbol, rather than that well-known scavenger, the bald eagle. However, neither the Pilgrims nor any other U.S. colonists—nor any gringos anywhere—ever managed to domesticate any subspecies of wild turkey. They tried repeatedly through the years. But problems with diseases that spread from one barnyard fowl to another, intensified

PEREGRINE FALCON, OREGON, FEBRUARY 1988

CALIFORNIA QUAIL, WASHINGTON,
APRIL 1989

social strife under confined conditions, and inbreeding sooner or later caused every scheme to collapse.

The trick of turkey domestication was apparently pulled off just once in history, sometime between the birth of Christ and A.D. 1000, by Indians in Mexico's central or northern highlands. Most likely, they were using *mexicana* for raw material. The taming may have been done by the Aztecs, since northern Mexico is where their legends say they were originally from. Or it may have been the work of another tribe that fell under the Aztec sphere of influence later on. Whatever the case, the Aztec empire was full of turkey pens. The birds were a crucial source of animal protein for early Mesoamericans, who relied upon maize for 90 percent of the calories in their diet. Their only other domestic animal of note was the hairless dog.

Turkeys were also a prime source of feathers for garments worn by the priest and warrior castes of both Maya and Aztec cultures. Aztec society included hereditary guilds of feather weavers, known as the *amanteca*. Their role was to fashion coats, cloaks, headgear, fans, and a steady supply of other adornments from hummingbirds prismatic as a sky god's rainbow; quetzals green as jade, green as the soft jungle light; and turkeys of more hues than you may imagine.

To refer to *Meleagris gallopavo* as the common turkey suggests that there might be uncommon turkeys out there somewhere. There are. They comprise the only other living turkey on the planet: *Agriocharis ocellata*, the ocellated turkey, indigenous to northern Central America. Two-thirds the size of the common turkey, the ocellated species is perhaps the most striking fowl in the hemisphere. It has a head of tropical blue ornamented by vivid red polyps of flesh—the caruncles—and body feathers of bronze and metallic green luster. And slate blue tailfeathers patterned, like a peacock's, by wide-awake aquamarine eyespots—the ocelli from which the bird takes its name. Somehow it escaped the notice of science until 1920, when it was reported from Honduras. Yet the feathers from wild populations of this polychrome turkey had been an important part of Mesoamerican civilizations for centuries.

Those civilizations were bound to birds in ways that we may never fathom. I see crowds gathered around their pyramids, garbed in avian plumage from head to toe, opening up the chests of human victims to lay still-beating hearts on the altar of the powerful, thirsty god Huitzilopochtli, the Hummingbird Wizard. I see them in their helmets shaped like beaks, paying homage to the Feathered Serpent, Quetzalcoatl. This central figure was both a deity and a cultural hero—a man who won immortality for his wisdom. The legends said he would come back one day, sailing home from across the sea. According to some sources, when Hernán Cortés and his conquistadors came ashore in 1519, many Aztecs were reluctant to drive him off because they conceived of him as the returning god.

Cortés found one of the finest aviaries in the world at the Aztecs' capital city, Tenochtitlán, displaying species from throughout the empire. By 1521 Cortés had brought down that empire and was shipping domesticated turkeys home to Spain. From there the birds spread through the rest of Europe. And from there they re-

The California quail (Callipepla californica) occupies the drier habitats available along the Pacific coast from Washington to Baja. Adapted to chaparral and scrub, it adjusts easily to logged-over pine forests, farmlands, and suburban areas, and it has been introduced by sportsmen to many other parts of the West and to Hawaii. In mountainous locales the California quail migrates between high elevation summer ranges and low altitude wintering areas, and it apparently does so by walking all the way. A gregarious species in winter, it forms flocks, or coveys, of up to two hundred birds, with occasional gatherings of three hundred. Good rainfall means good production of young in this and other quail species; low rainfall, low reproduction. In part rainfall determines the abundance of a favored type of food—legumes, which have a high protein content. Low rainfall not only means less high-quality food, it also causes some of the leguminous plants that are available to build up concentrations of chemicals called phytoestrogens. These are compounds similar to those that birds and mammals produce themselves to regulate reproduction. High levels of phytoestrogens, which may have evolved as part of the plants' chemical defense against heavy grazing by large mammals, result in markedly lower egg production among quail.

turned to the Americas with the colonists of what was to be the United States, keeping regular company now with the likes of horses, goats, pigs, and chickens—domesticated from Asian jungle fowl. Wherever they are found in the world these days, domestic turkeys still have the white-tipped tailfeathers that characterize *mexicana*, ancestor of all the plump Thanksgiving centerpieces with which we unfailingly stuff ourselves.

Conservationists regularly point out that in saving an obscure life form in the wild, we may be preserving the genetic basis from which people could develop a valuable crop or type of livestock. That could still be the case for the ocellated turkey, which has become exceedingly rare over most of its former range. In the case of the Mexican turkey our Rancho Pallan group was trying to preserve an obscure subspecies that had already given rise to a domesticated animal of considerable economic importance.

To shorten a long story *los guajalotes* finally came into our traps. And then everything that could possibly go wrong certainly did, and at the worst possible moment. Which I suppose sums up quite a lot about not only our turkey-trapping outfit but the U.S. Army, much of human history, and possibly the nature of the universe. Perhaps it also explains why people find it necessary to spend so much time at prayer.

Our foolproof drop nets fooled everyone except the turkeys by dropping late. Troops charged into the fray in full camouflage dress, fumbling birds between them like loose footballs, while the explosive devices designed to drop the nets finally went off like grenades, adding to the confusion. At least we had a few birds caught beneath the net. Back at Fort Huachuca, where technicians chart test results of the latest infraquantum technolaser zapbeam capable of sneaking around corners to turn enemy lungs inside out, the troops had painstakingly woven these nets by hand over a period of months. There was no way that the struggling birds were going to get loose given the strength of the material and the size of the mesh. Yet here they were, suddenly altering the laws of physics through techniques known only to very desperate wild Mexican turkeys, rearranging their bodies into impossible shapes and squeezing through the mesh in some places, tearing it apart in other places, gobbling like hell, and exploding into the air in a shower of feathers above the lurching camouflage uniforms and grasping hands.

Over by our cannon-fired net a guy who had huddled cold and cramped all morning in his camouflaged blind finally crawled out to relieve his bowels—and some toms that no one had noticed approaching the net instantly spotted him and sped away, squawking to themselves. Even simple box traps malfunctioned in incredibly complex ways.

We eventually caught seventeen birds. As far as anyone could tell, every single one of them was a hen. Looking over our strange haul on the day we were leaving, a local *vaquero* took a drag on his cigarette and shook his head slowly, muttering something in Spanish.

"What's he saying?"

GRAY WOLF, ALASKA, AUGUST 1987

"He says he doesn't know what all these *guajalotas* are supposed to do for a husband."

The answer is nothing. They might as well have been sterile. The teams planned to converge on Rancho Pallan the next year for another try, but the paperwork once again delayed any honest work until the mixed flocks began to break up for the breeding season. The year after that, the chief Mexican biologist left for another job. Then key Army personnel were transferred. The last news I had was that the transplant project was indefinitely on hold.

Our turkey foray left me with two persistent thoughts. First, to save a species or subspecies in trouble, we must provide more than the minimum habitat, money, manpower, or whatever is required. We must come up with an extra measure—some slack—to account for bad luck. Hurricanes in the last forests set aside for the red-cockaded woodpeckers of the Southeast, for instance. Disease in the black-footed ferret population that was discovered in Wyoming after the species had been all but written off as extinct, for another example. Unhappily, even the minimum is more than we seem to be able to scrabble together for many creatures.

And that brings up the second thought, which has to do with how haphazardly we go about preserving endangered species in general. Granted our U.S. Army incursion into Mexican territory was not a typical program. But it was typically less than what was called for in order to ensure a successful result. Nationwide and kingdom-wide, our efforts remain equally unreliable. Despite the endangered species regulations intended to lend some degree of consistency to our efforts, the matter of which life forms we actually choose to protect and how seriously we go about protecting them still depends upon far too many arbitrary factors: the influence of local industries, the favors owed powerful congressmen, the energy and organizational skills of individual conservationists, the mood of the populace and the sort of wildlife it happens to perceive as valuable or endearing at any given moment, the current state of the economy and changes in funding for various agencies. The entire endangered species program is periodically threatened with extinction itself. It is tough enough just having to contend with bad luck.

Consider the incredibly detailed systems analysis—double and triple checks of each tiny component—through which NASA proceeds toward the lift-off of a single space vehicle. Now compare that to the way in which we attend to the working parts of our planetary spaceship. Right. And this is our one and only life support system, dependent upon the cellular technology and architecture of organisms.

The community of living things traveling along with us amounts to a vast and miraculous library of knowledge accumulated throughout the planet's history. The genetic material contained within each species represents a unique volume on how to create, say, wings. Or glistening membranes, thorns, pads, armor, petals. Healing balms, poisons, poison neutralizers. Adaptations to unusual atmospheric conditions or submarine environments. Sonar receptors. Spiraling shells. A morning song. Phosphorescent fin colors. Or eyes that seem to shine through the darkness. At the

116

RUFFED GROUSE, WYOMING, NOVEMBER 1989

SNOW GEESE, BOSQUE DEL APACHE NATIONAL WILDLIFE REFUGE, NEW MEXICO, FEBRUARY 1987

same time, as others have pointed out, these other beings may well be our only companions for many and many a galaxy.

Not that there isn't a certain charm and drama in the way we go about trying to save our fellow voyagers and their genetic codes: the mixture of volunteers and a few dedicated public servants stretching out shoestring budgets and patching the gaps with faith; the alarms, propaganda, and public posturings; then the hard-nosed political infighting; and finally the poignant rescues and last-minute stays of extinction—sometimes. But sometimes not. We aren't always getting the job done in time. We aren't getting it done right. Too many environmental crises are building too fast, and we've had too many failures even when the pace was slower. This is simply no way to run a spaceship, a kingdom, or anything else.

We need to be able to count on something more. Something methodical, long-term, large-scale, bountifully funded, and without any room for bias. We need an unshakable commitment by our governing bodies, on the order of our commitment to the ideals of democracy and human dignity, to maintain the living processes of this realm. There is no more important heritage to be kept for the future. There is no more important work at hand. The world has reached a point at which the only sensible thing for each of us to do, and the only honorable thing—the only thing that really counts at all—is to help save it. Every hair. Every radiant feather. Every piece.

At the very least it is something you might contemplate while sitting down at the table next Thanksgiving—maybe when the time comes to say grace.

Snow geese (Chen caerulescens) breed in tundra realms far from human crowds. But their winter ranges are much closer to civilization, as at Bosque del Apache National Wildlife Refuge on the upper Rio Grande, where some thirty thousand snow geese congregate. Like many waterfowl, wintering snow geese make frequent daytime forays from marshlands to cropfields in the surrounding area.

PYGMY OWL, WASHINGTON, SEPTEMBER 1988

CHAPTER SIX
The Woodrat

WOODRATS don't really look like rats. Their ears are large, their coats plush, their tails bushy as squirrels'. They are closer kin to gerbils and lemmings than to rats, which belong to a different rodent family. Woodrats do live in the woods. And also in high mountain cliff country, deserts, and scrublands. The one I got to know best inhabited Revenue Flats, a sagebrush benchland partway up the west slope of Montana's Madison Valley. For its nest site the woodrat had chosen the attic of an abandoned miner's shack there. The building was still sound and mostly dry. That was why I moved in downstairs one summer long ago.

In the late 1800s when Revenue Flats was a bustling gold camp, someone lined the cabin walls with newspapers to keep out drafts. The sheets had held up well. I liked to sidestep along them catching up on old news of wars and crimes, along with advertisements for uncomfortable-looking clothes and elixirs promising to make everyone feel better. Near one wall stood a workbench with my beetle collection. I was in my late teens, and an enthusiastic naturalist. My goal was to keep catching, pinning, and labeling various beetles until I came up with a new species—or at least one not yet known from Montana. As the summer wore on I got seriously distracted from my bug work by cowgirls. But then I hadn't come to Revenue Flats for bugs anyway. I was sampling, surveying, and drilling rock as an assistant to my father, a geologist. His goal was to determine whether or not this old mining area abandoned to woodrats and the weather was worth tunneling into for precious metal again.

Woodrats are also fond of treasures. Like the bowerbirds of New Guinea and people of every sort, they decorate their dwellings with bright, attractive objects: shiny stones, small bones, pieces of plastic or foil, sometimes a coin or two. They also cache berries, buds, cones, and other food. Hence the name pack rats. Since they may drop whatever they happen to be carrying along in their large cheek pouches in order to pick up something more intriguing, they also go by the name of trade rats. Working in Arizona during an earlier summer, I heard tales of Spanish doubloons hoarded in pack rat nests. I began to poke through those large mounds of piled twigs whenever I came across one. I quit after scratching my way into a cactus-shielded nest that hid not riches but rattlesnake. Big, angry rattlesnake. It had probably been prospecting for young woodrats.

With a wingspread of up to four and a half inches and a long tail on each of the hind wings, the luna moth (Actias luna) is an unmistakable species. It belongs to the family of giant silkworm moths, the Saturniidae. These are not closely related to the Asiatic silkworm, but the luna moth caterpillar does spin a strong yet flexible, silky cocoon, which usually lies loose on the ground among fallen leaves. The luna moth is most often seen in the eastern half of the continent from southern Canada into Mexico. In the caterpillar stage it eats the leaves of hickory, sweet gum, persimmon, birch, walnut, and several other trees. As an adult it does not feed at all. It has only remnant mouthparts, and exists in this striking winged form for only a very short time, to mate and then to die. Similar saturnids are found on other continents, but Actias luna is an exclusively North American species. Unfortunately, pesticides and pollutants have made it an endangered one.

Archeologists study prehistoric cultures by poking around in their garbage dumps. These waste piles, known as middens, are often located just outside the entrance of caves. Many woodrats nest in caves and crevices, creating middens of their own. Generation after generation adds to the heap of woodrat knickknacks and leftover groceries, all cemented together and preserved with resinlike dried urine and excrement. Such gunk is the paleobotanist's gold—a fossil lode of seeds and woody tissues that can reveal what the local plant community was like in bygone centuries, sometimes as far back as the end of the Ice Age. According to the woodrats much of what is now sagebrush country used to grow towering sequoias and bristlecone pines.

Around the sagebrush-scented ghost camp of Revenue Flats, the woodrat-human relationship came down to this: most nights I would hear scurryings. Sometimes there were odd tappings as well, because woodrats thump a hind leg when they are agitated, much as rabbits do. And in the morning I would be missing something. Especially equipment from my beetle table. Tweezers. My small magnifying glass. Pieces of white paper. Although none of my beetles got crunched, a green-shelled specimen with the metallic luster of jewelry disappeared upstairs. How many times did some Shoshone or Bannock Indian camp here before the miners came, get up, greet the sun, look around, and notice woodrat tracks where a favorite bead or obsidian arrowhead had been? One night I watched the bushy-tailed beast try to drag my checkered flannel shirt through a hole it had gnawed earlier in the boards. Now and then I found a woodrat gift in exchange. A slender bird bone. Maybe a chip of ore from the old mine dump. We got along all right with this barter system. I could always climb to the attic and retrieve whatever I needed from the nest.

Midway through the summer one of the drill crew struck a streak of gold during his off-hour explorations. The guy quit his job cold, and, with a kind of hypnotized expression, went forth to attack the metal-bearing quartz vein with pick and shovel. The drill boss shrugged and said to wait it out, as if he were dealing with a hired hand on a drinking binge. Gold fever and whiskey fever can be hard to tell apart, and a man has to figure them out for himself. The driller piled up his ore from several days' mining, crushed it with a hammer, washed it in a gold pan, and weighed out the yellow dust—the color, the fines. He finally realized that he was making about half of what he had on the drill crew per hour, though he was working ten times as hard. He slunk back to his regular occupation. No one said anything more on the subject. It was about that time that I awakened around midnight with a weight on my chest. The weight was the woodrat, perched there studying my face.

Two nights later the woodrat was back on my chest. It stayed even as I slowly reached out and switched on a bedside flashlight. It stayed—and kept peering straight at me. The eyes reflected red. At the stroke of midnight you can easily convince yourself that a woodrat is the ghost of some long-gone miner, a shaman, a friendly imp with some magic to share, or a messenger from the devil. Or anything else you like, depending upon what sort of mood your dreams have left you in. Even-

ELK, YELLOWSTONE NATIONAL PARK, MONTANA, NOVEMBER 1989

YOUNG OPOSSUMS, WASHINGTON, JUNE 1988

tually, I said, "What's up?" My visitor leaped away. Yet the question stuck with me. What is up with this rodent? What does it want?

Several nights passed. Then, once more, the attic dweller came to sit on me in the wee hours, with its ruby eyes and bristling whisker antennae. It came to. . . . What? Satisfy some sort of woodrat curiosity? Open some sort of woodrat dialogue? Why, I began wondering, is it so difficult to know what is real and what is not about animal motives? Why are we at such a loss for ways to understand their thoughts and feelings? Time and again we stand at a threshold and have no sure way to proceed.

On the one hand we get mired in storybook images, describing other species as if they were humans with especially cute or ferocious personalities—people dressed up in animal suits. This is the usual anthropomorphic approach. It comes naturally, and such impressions can sometimes lead straight to the heart of a universal animal quality. As a rule, though, they reveal more about human sentiments and the moral judgments of a particular culture than about wild lives. For every person inspired to save creatures that he or she perceives as cuddly or noble, there is another person who speaks of bad animals—vicious, skulking, ugly, greedy, or just plain bothersome members of the wild kingdom—and feels righteous about destroying their kind.

At the other extreme we confine animals to the hard cage of science. Ethology, the study of animal behavior, is a field I admire and have practiced. Still it is a reductive approach, inclined to analyze the most subtle and suggestive activities of our fellow creatures in terms of stimulus-response patterns. Nonhumans are automatons until proven otherwise. With few exceptions the subjects are assumed to have neither complex emotional needs nor powers of reason, much less the sort of interaction between the two that we ourselves often struggle with.

I suppose it is only good science to ascribe to animals no more than those abilities of which we can be absolutely sure. But how do we tell when an animal is capable of something that we aren't yet capable of even beginning to translate? In other words, how do we know whether the limitation is in the animal or in ourselves? What do we really know about the causes of our own behavior? I don't understand why the sight of mountains arrayed against the sky or the trajectory of a single bird above the plains moves me so. And yet I live for these things.

Ethology offers itself as an antidote to anthropomorphism. But it relies so heavily upon an elaborate jargon, formal logic, and mechanistic models that it may at times reveal more about the nature of human thought patterns and Western intellectual traditions in particular, than about the essence of animals. In short it, too, can be a form of anthropomorphism.

We seem to keep looking out upon the world and describing ourselves. That isn't *seeing*, and it isn't communicating. Since meeting the Revenue Flats woodrat, I've wanted to find out what is.

The central problem, I think, is that our society has never decided what its relationship to other beings is or ought to be. We have not yet found common ground. Perhaps this is because we aren't yet ready to admit that there really is such a shared

The presence of the Virginia opossum (Didelphis virginiana) in North America speaks of a time when portions of the American land mass were joined to that of Australia, and mammalian fauna was dominated by marsupials. After a gestation period of only about two weeks a brood of twenty or more bee-size opossum babies emerge from the female's vulva. Still essentially fetuses, they squirm and pull their way up her fur to reach the belly pouch, or marsupium. There they compete to attach themselves to thirteen nipples. Losers perish. Winners remain attached to this milk line for the next two months. They continue suckling for another hundred days, but come and go from the pouch during that time, often riding on their mother's back. Opossums do not hibernate, but their level of activity drops during cold weather. Their dens are lined with leaves that may be carried in the animal's prehensile tail while the paws are used for climbing. Since colonial times the Virginia opossum appears to have extended its range northward into New England and southern Ontario. Whether this is a result of climatic change or human-caused habitat changes is difficult to say. Opossums suffer from frostbite on their ears and tails toward the northern limits of their range, and heavy die-offs have been recorded there in harsh winters. This omnivorous species has proven adept at exploiting whatever food is available, from wild grasses, berries, insects, frogs, mice, and even poisonous pit vipers to chicken eggs and garbage around human settlement.

127

Swiftest of all North American land mammals, the pronghorn (Antilocapra americana) can attain speeds of more than fifty miles per hour. Perhaps because it senses that it can outpace almost any danger, the pronghorn is given to approaching predators, such as coyotes, and any strange or curious objects within its homeland. Hunters will sometimes hide behind a bush or boulder and wave a handkerchief to lure this inquisitive hoofed animal closer. Pronghorns are commonly called antelope, but they are unrelated to the true antelope of Africa and Asia. Instead they are the sole member of the family Antilocapridae, unique to North America. The pronghorn is the only living ungulate on the continent that arose and evolved here. All the others, from musk-oxen to moose, originated in Eurasia and crossed to the New World during the Ice Age. As in the bovid family, whose members include true antelope, cattle, goats, and sheep, pronghorns carry horns made of keratin—the same protein that forms hair and nails—growing over a bony core. But unlike any bovids, pronghorns shed their horns annually. In males the horns are large and branched. Females carry smaller, simpler horns. Pronghorns also possess a unique array of scent glands below the ear, on the rump, and even between the toes. These are used during courtship displays and to mark territory. The bright white hairs of the rump patch can be raised to become even more conspicuous, serving as a distant warning signal to other pronghorns in the area.

sphere of needs to consider. Not enough of us want the responsibility. Our guiding philosophies reinforce the idea that we are wonderfully special, wonderfully apart. Why shouldn't we project ourselves out upon the world? It is ours for the taking.

We've done pretty well thinking that way in the past. So well that the world holds at least ten times as many people as it did when most of our religious and ethical beliefs were formulated. And now we are changing the forests, rangelands, soils, groundwater reservoirs, the very seas and atmosphere at a rate that places enormous pressures upon every plant and animal community, including our own. None will prosper once the environment deteriorates past a certain point, and that is perhaps the most fundamental aspect of common ground. It is time to explore the other aspects—*before* the ecosystems we share become damaged beyond repair. A continent of life depends upon us gaining new vision.

Who will help us break out of our old patterns? Who can render advice? Offer an outside opinion? When you can go no farther by yourself, you turn to the people closest to you. When the counsel of people isn't enough, we have to go on to the next closest thing. My hope lies with the animals. Each is a survival expert with a great deal to teach us about how to live in North American landscapes. The more we open ourselves to their ways, the better we can see the world around us through their eyes. Maybe one day we'll be able to see it whole.

The Tobacco Root Mountains above Revenue Flats hold a lot of naked rock and snowfields up against the sky. On my free days I often rambled the high basins among boulder fields, tundra meltlakes, summer elk, and eagles. Pine forests follow the mountainsides down to drier elevations and then finger out onto ridgelines while scattered juniper take over the side hills. In the draws flow springs and beaver-dammed streams sheltered by glades of quaking aspen, my favorite sort of place to spend time below the peaks. Aspen catch the mountain sunlight and mill it between their trembling, silver-bottomed leaves until it grows soft. Then they spread the glow evenly onto the deer beds and wild geraniums underneath. Even the shadows there are a luminous green. And the flower pollen trapped in the fine hairs of beetles glimmers like gold dust. In the foothills the streams are edged by willow instead, and they run between open stretches of sagebrush and bunchgrass until they join the Madison River.

The Madison begins up on the Yellowstone Plateau. It comes out laden with minerals from hot springs, winter-killed bison, and the droppings of trumpeter swans. This solution dances with stoneflies and smells like big trout. And at Three Forks it meets the waters of the Gallatin and Jefferson to begin the Missouri River. Nearly every evening at Revenue Flats, I would climb up onto a stone outcrop and sit a while just to watch the distant Madison shine. To me this river is a distillation of all the good juices of the Rockies, bound across the continent for the Mississippi. Sometimes in the sunset light I thought about getting in a canoe and following the Madison on to the salty Gulf of Mexico. Sometimes I thought about woodrats.

The woodrat stopped its nighttime studies of me as abruptly as it started them. A

PRONGHORN, WYOMING, NOVEMBER 1989

SNOWY EGRET, FLORIDA,
JANUARY 1989

couple of weeks later, I was dangling on a rope nearly a hundred feet down in a vertical mine shaft, sampling the stone at intervals by flashlight, when the woodrat joined me. These rodents are expert climbers and regularly scale sheer-looking cliffs by gripping small irregularities with their nimble paws. So my companion's descent was not extraordinary in itself. As for what it was doing there, I had no idea. The shaft was some distance from the cabin, yet still, I suppose, within the woodrat's foraging range. It might have had another nest or food cache somewhere in the mine. It was definitely the same individual. An ear tattered by battle, infection, or maybe frostbite marked it well enough. And it perched on a ledge within arm's length to stare at me the same way it did when perched on my chest. Fearless. Questioning, I thought. For all I know our encounter here came about completely by chance. Maybe the rodent was just entertaining itself. But I couldn't shake the feeling that this trade rat was offering me something I didn't know how to receive. I never saw or heard the animal again. Never—though I found myself drawn to that attic and the mine from time to time, searching for the acquaintance that had existed between us.

During the breeding season the snowy egret (Egretta thula) *performs its territorial and sexual displays with the aid of particularly long and lovely feathers that develop on its head, neck, and breast, and also down its back. Other egrets have similar special nuptial plumes, known as aigrettes. The birds are named after them. Aigrettes also became important in the displays of fashionable women, who adorned their hats with these feathers. During its height around the turn of the century, the plume trade involved at least sixty-four native avian species. It all but obliterated many of the great wading birds. Since protective measures were passed, the snowy egret rebounded to a point where it even exceeded its precolonial range, expanding into portions of the northeastern United States. But its numbers have once again begun to decline, this time as a result of wetland habitat losses to development.*

PORCUPINE, IDAHO, JUNE 1988

ELK, YELLOWSTONE NATIONAL PARK, WYOMING, JANUARY 1989

SNOW GEESE, WESTERN WASHINGTON, DECEMBER 1989

CHAPTER SEVEN

Home

Tʜɪs ʙᴏᴏᴋ's first chapter is set on the eastern edge of the Continental Divide in Montana, along the Rocky Mountain Front. My home lies just over the mountains from the Front, on the Divide's western slope. Of the few roads that cross that way in northern Montana, the finest leads through the core of Glacier National Park. It follows a trail used by the Blackfeet when they went west to raid the Flathead-Salish tribes. And it was used by the Flathead-Salish when they traveled east to reap buffalo from the prairies. The route winds up and up through shadowed valleys swept by moving beams of light. Up to the realm of little trees and ptarmigan meadows. And up among the mineral geometries of the peaks, where parts of the sky spread underfoot and brightness echoes like a war cry. The Indian name for this path is Going-to-the-Sun.

To the south of the pass juts Triple Divide Peak, whose snowmelt runs east down the Missouri to the Atlantic, west down the Columbia to the Pacific, and north down the Saskatchewan to Hudson Bay and the Arctic Ocean. From the north side of the pass rises a blade-edge ridge called the Garden Wall. Its snowmelt percolates through talus fields to spray out of the roadcut onto the Going-to-the-Sun highway, baptizing cars that pass along the inside lane. Not far beyond the Weeping Wall, as this section is called, you sometimes get snagged in a high-country traffic jam: Dozens of vehicles sit abandoned in the middle of the road while their owners trot back and forth pointing fingers, cameras, video gear, and children's heads at the steep cliff face just overhead. Up there, staring back, stands a mountain goat, balanced on a thin ledge at the very edge of the air.

Many of the tourists have the impression that the animal is at risk of tumbling off its perch. The mountain goat does not think so. If it did, it would be crouched, its tail up and its tongue probably flicking in and out of its mouth every so often. This one merely continues to study the people. Then it nonchalantly lifts a hind leg from its hold on the precipice to scratch along its neck. Murmurs of astonishment rise from the crowd. You can sense that underneath the buzz of transitory thoughts about did I remember to set the parking brake and what speed of film did Ethel say she put in here, other, older kinds of questions are taking form.

From one big-brained creature to another, both of them caught up in the interlocking puzzle of existence: What are you doing up there? How do you go day after day without a fatal slip? And then year after year, rearing your babies and struggling

The distinctive black tips on the wings of snow geese (Chen caerulescens) show up clearly in flight. Not long ago birdwatchers often spoke about a similar species known as the blue goose. Today it is recognized as a color phase of the snow goose. Flocks containing both phases are fairly common. Although these birds may assume the V-formation typical of geese aloft, they often break up into irregular patterns, in part because the snow goose flies in a more undulating, up-and-down style than other species. Scientists are still debating the value of flying in V-formation in the first place. The consensus used to be that it was a matter of subtle aerodynamics—that flying at an angle behind the goose in front somehow offered extra lift. At the moment many feel that the V-formation may simply be the best way for a group of big waterfowl that are not especially agile in midair to avoid collisions while keeping in close contact. Before departing for the winter, snow geese may collect en masse on the tundra, stripping the low vegetation of seeds and ripe berries. They also stop off at regular staging areas on their way south. By traveling in flocks with more experienced birds, young geese on their first journey can learn details of the traditional migration route, though no one can prove that geographic features are really what the animals use to guide their way. As with flying formations, the mysteries of navigation are still far from completely solved.

The weasel, or mustelid, family's members range in size from the least weasel—the world's smallest carnivore, weighing only a couple of ounces—to the sea otter, which may weigh up to a hundred pounds. The marten (Martes americana) is about the size of a cat. Its main prey is the squirrel. But it will take mice, voles, shrews, chipmunks, hares, birds and their eggs, bugs, and, when ripe, nuts and berries. When food grows scarce, its normal home range area of one or two square miles may expand to fifteen square miles. Closely tied to mature, northern conifer forests, martens have lost a good deal of ground to logging and settlement. These fur-bearers are quite easy to trap, and unregulated trapping further reduced populations in decades past. So did the poisons put out as part of programs to eradicate predators. Wildlife managers have achieved some success in restoring martens to a few areas, but intensive logging throughout more and more of the backcountry continues to elimi-nate prime forest habitat faster than it can regrow.

to outlast the winters? How did a tribe such as yours come to exist in the first place at the uppermost limit of life? And what are you thinking while you look at me? What's behind that bright eye at the border of heaven and earth?

Asking more or less the same sort of questions in a systematic way, I studied mountain goats for seven years as a wildlife biologist. I began my research into their behavior and ecology at the western edge of the Bob Marshall Wilderness, then moved on to Glacier National Park. The scientific background, I already possessed. The necessary survival skills, I had to pick up as I went along; some of them directly from the goats and their neighbors. At times I lived with the goat herds for months on end, and I stayed in their high homeland through the snowbound seasons as well as during the ephemeral summers. When I was through, I wanted a home of my own. On reasonably level ground, and in a sheltering place. I only looked in two areas, though: near the edge of the Bob Marshall Wilderness and near the edge of Glacier National Park. I had a pretty definite idea of what the backyard should be like.

My wife, Karen Reeves, and I searched for months, never quite finding a piece of property that invited us to stay. One midwinter day driving through Kalispell, Mon-tana, the central town of the Flathead Valley, we noticed yet another office that said Real Estate. This one was located in a used car lot. The salesman told us of a parcel of land in the remote North Fork of the Flathead River Valley near the park's western boundary. Judging from the downtown cut of his clothes, he was not going to be en-thusiastic about guiding us. In fact, he never offered. He sketched the route on a scrap of paper and waved goodbye through the falling snow from his rows of cars and slush.

The farther north we drove, the faster the snow fell, until we were weaving and slipping in two feet of fresh flakes past bands of ghost deer. We ground along in first gear for a spell behind a moose that was reluctant to leave the road for the deeper snow on either side. Finally, a few hundred feet past a pair of coyotes, the turnoff to the property appeared. We strapped on snowshoes and were soon moving through gentle, riverine country that was a mixture of meadow and forest. The forest itself was a mixture of conifers, cottonwoods, and aspen. After a short while the storm be-gan easing a bit, and we came to a weathered shack near the edge of the river channel. The land for sale was originally part of an old homestead. The husband and wife who owned the property at the moment lived in town. This little chunk of the North Fork was their weekend place, where the husband liked to do some hunting with a couple of friends, sip some whiskey, play some cards—and every so often, when he wanted to raise some cash, go out and fell some more timber.

Just before putting the land up for sale, the man cut nearly all the merchantable trees that he hadn't got around to in earlier years. The ground was rubbled with stumps and piled high with slash—leftover treetops and limbs—to be burned. It would look like hell come spring, when the snow melted down to trails of torn earth where the logs had been skidded. Yet gauzed over with snow the scene didn't seem bad, and I could envision how quickly this moist bottomland would heal itself with

PINE MARTEN, WASHINGTON, JANUARY 1987

The usual nest for the great gray owl (Strix nebulosa) is one abandoned by an eagle or hawk. When these owls build a nest of their own, it is often placed where a tree trunk has broken off and left a stump fairly high off the ground. For weeks after they are able to fly the owlets still return to their nest to roost. They will stay with their parents for several months before departing to try life on their own. Voles are this owl's preferred prey, in part because voles are frequently active during daylight hours and the great gray is largely diurnal as well. The majority of owls are, of course, nocturnal, along with the majority of small mammals, from mice to rabbits. A hunter of the taiga and northern boreal forests, the great gray owl also ranges southward along the Rockies and the Cascades. It is the largest owl in North America; its wings span a distance of five feet.

the help of a little cleaning and a few summers' warmth. Besides, right across the river channel, on a long island consisting of state and national forest land, were spruce and cottonwood monuments to more than four hundred years of uninterrupted growth.

And then in the channel itself: "Doggone if there isn't some gold," the realtor from the car lot had informed us. "The old boy used to pan for it in his spare time, I believe. Wouldn't surprise me if a guy was able to make some pretty fair money if he wanted to get serious about the whole deal." I remember grinning at the realtor and deciding that I was probably not going to buy one of his used automobiles.

This used land, however, was another matter. It felt good. The channel's banks were covered with signatures of wild animals laying claim to its course. Where the river was running, the water was utterly transparent—a clarification of each tiny pebble and conifer needle on the bottom. Many of those were cemented together into tubular protective cases by the abundant caddis fly larvae tracing fine tracks in the silt. Where the river was frozen over, the snow and ice were freshly marked by otter bellies. Pad pad pad glide. Pad pad pad pad gliiiide. The pattern looked like animal code for everyday delight. Then a slight detour and fresh droppings, which said that the otter family's bellies were full of caddis fly larvae.

Fog settled in as the snowfall ended. Continuing upstream, we saw beaver chisel-work everywhere. Even some cottonwoods whose trunks two people could not have joined arms around had been gnawed through. A small but noteworthy percentage of the time such trees are found lying on their sides with squashed beavers underneath them. Which probably explains why beavers stick to smaller timber and shrubs as a rule.

Beavers' large, bright orange incisor teeth grow continuously to compensate for wear, and the upper pair overlap the lower pair just slightly where they meet so that there is a constant self-sharpening effect on the cutting edges. The animals' dung on pond bottoms resembles soggy particle board, because the animals take in a fair amount of indigestible material in the course of scraping off their main food items: buds, bark, and the underlying cambium layer—the woody plants' nutrient-laden transport system. These rodents, which can weigh anywhere from thirty pounds to nearly seventy pounds as adults, then work the stripped sticks into the construction of their lodges and dams, being one of those species that engineers much of its own habitat. For plaster they use mud and muck. At times they might add nearby rocks to help shore up a dam, just as they often use rocks to weigh down cut branches on the bottom of the pool as a winter food cache. What I did not know until I walked this North Fork land in search of a home was that at least one group of beavers builds its impoundments entirely from rock.

The North Fork channel is naturally paved with smooth, rounded stones that were shaped first by the glaciers and thereafter by the river's flow. Selecting mainly those between the size of a baseball and a soccer ball, the beavers had assembled perfect masonry dikes at intervals across the current, rolling the rocks into place with their

GREAT GRAY OWLS, OREGON, JUNE 1985

GREAT BLUE HERON ROOKERY, WESTERN WASHINGTON, APRIL 1989

paws. Three to four feet wide and two to three feet high, some of these structures spanned sixty feet or more. A few had a garnish of sticks interwoven along the surface, but the essential construction remained mud mortar and stone upon stone. I wonder whether this is a local genetic trait or a learned behavior. I also wonder what this particular stone-age beaver culture might do with a load of bricks.

Having a pool behind a dam enables beavers to escape predators by submerging and to transport food by floating branches rather than having to drag them. At the same time the reservoir encourages a future grocery supply of willow, red-osier dogwood, birch, and aspen, all of which will invade newly created marshes. In backing up water for their own purposes beavers simultaneously create habitats for pond and marshland dwellers from moose to ducks and salamanders. A series of beaver dams stores spring runoff and rainwater, preserving some flow for the hot summer months and times of drought, when creeks might otherwise run dry. Thus the cooperative busyness of big, buck-toothed, paddle-tailed rodents spills over to benefit a wide array of water-dependent species downstream. Trout and crayfish would be two obvious examples. Farmers and ranchers would be two more.

In parts of the American Southwest stream courses now parched, eroded by flash floods, and bordered by cactus once flowed year-round, silver-shadowed with trout, through cool hardwood forests. But that was during the previous century before commercial fur trapping eliminated beavers and their dams, beginning a process of lowering the water table that was soon accelerated by overgrazing and settlement. The key role of beavers in conserving North America's water and wetlands reaches back much earlier. Certain large ripples in the landscape that long mystified geologists are now believed to be the remains of dams built by Ice Age beavers—serious engineers the size of bears. The fertile soil of some modern agricultural lands represents the sediments that accumulated behind such prehistoric impoundments.

Along the North Fork channel the willow and dogwood bushes not cut by beavers were pruned by the regular browsing of hoofed animals. Some of the tallest bushes were broken where moose had straddled them with their forelegs and then walked forward until the stems snapped against their chests, bringing branches that had been out of reach down to moose mouth level. Elk and white-tailed deer had been feeding on the slimmer bushes. Their tracks converged toward the island of old-growth forest and coalesced beneath the great trees.

Large, fully mature conifers, such as the spruce flourishing on these bottomlands, intercept a great deal of snowfall on their tightly layered evergreen branches. The dark mass of the tree also absorbs and stores such heat as the winter sun offers. Underneath, then, you may find a space the size of a hut's interior virtually free of snow and slightly warmer than the surrounding air. Its value as shelter for wintering wildlife is plain from the concentration of tracks and dung. During cold snaps I, too, have spent many nights with a spruce between me and the subzero dark, watching my campfire light dance within the blue-green embrace of the branches.

When the snowpack starts to pile up several feet high, the long-legged moose can

Sometimes a pair of great blue herons (Ardea herodias) will nest by themselves. More often they nest with others in rookeries. These may occur on cliff sides, but a typical rookery is built in the branches of tall trees. Where they nest in mixed groups with other wading birds, the herons usually occupy the upper branches. Eventually the excrement that accumulates beneath traditional rookeries kills the trees. This presents a problem for some populations along the East Coast, where development has already removed huge tracts of great blue heron nesting habitat. At the nest, built of interwoven sticks and lined with smaller twigs and leaves, pairs clap their long mandibles together during both courtship and territorial defense displays, making a hollow sound that carries for some distance. Three eggs are usually laid, often two or three days apart, and both sexes take turns incubating them. Larger clutches are produced in more northerly ranges, with Canadian heron nests holding an average of five eggs. No matter what the clutch size, the earliest chicks born tend to destroy their younger siblings, robbing them of food and stabbing them with sharp bills. The parents could not really afford to keep a large brood fed, anyway. The extra eggs are "insurance" against loss of the clutch due to harsh weather, predators, or some other cause.

141

Once widespread throughout the Americas, the cougar (Felis concolor) is today primarily an animal of remote mountainous terrain in the West. An adult male weighs between 150 and 230 pounds, just slightly smaller than the continent's largest feline, the jaguar. The cats are pure predators, powerful and efficient, with exceptionally sharp, well-developed canine teeth. They hunt mainly through stealth and generally at night, aided by eyes that are the largest among carnivores in relation to body size. The cougar's prey may be as small as rabbits or as large as elk. This carnivore has its best success hunting hoofed animals during winter, when deep snow confines the ungulates to limited ranges and makes escape more difficult. Like its fellow cats, the cougar almost never scavenges carcasses, preferring fresh meat. And it favors choice muscle tissue, generally avoiding internal organs, tendons, and bones. Specialized teeth called carnassials are designed for shearing off chunks of flesh, while the tongue, with its rasplike pattern of sharp bristles, is specialized for licking meat clean from the bone. Breeding may take place at any time of year, but usually occurs in winter or early spring among northern cougar populations. Outside of this two-week period of association between males and females, adult cougars remain strictly apart from one another. But the young, numbering between one and six per litter, may stay with their mother for almost two years.

142

still muscle through it from shrub to shrub to put together a full meal. But elk and, particularly, deer rely more and more upon trails tramped out beneath stands of old-growth trees to travel from one feeding site to another. Without such natural roofing in heavy winter country it becomes that much tougher for some animals to deal with winter's nagging question: Can you take in enough food calories to match the energy used up seeking that food and keeping warm? If the answer is no for too many days on end, you lose your fat reserves, then your muscle tissue, and finally your life.

At the same time sections of young, or secondary, forest are also vital to animals such as elk and deer. More of the grasses, herbs, and shrubs that sustain them spring up once heavy tree cover has been removed, letting in sunlight for growth in the understory. Fires open the forest canopy this way. So do floods, windstorms, avalanches and landslides, outbreaks of certain insects, and epidemics of various tree diseases. And beavers. And logging. The timber industry makes much of this relationship, arguing that more cutting means more wildlife. They refer to old-growth not as mature but as overmature, or stagnant, unproductive, even decadent. Essentially going to waste.

On certain slopes at certain elevations timber harvesting can alter habitat in ways that benefit certain kinds of birds and mammals; no doubt about it. Logging also helps sustain a lot of humans. However, neither fact justifies clearcuts that are too large, as they often are, or too close together, in remnant woodlands that have become more important for refuge and shelter than for food, or on sites better left intact to conserve fragile soils, water quality, fisheries, and special scenic or recreational values. Meanwhile other types of plants and animals simply thrive best in primary, or old-growth, woodlands to begin with. Whether they be orchids in tropical rainforests or spotted owls in the rainforests of the Pacific Northwest, such species can only decline as the percentage of undisturbed forest does.

For decades timber management has been practiced as a variation on farming. The guiding philosophy is that forests are renewable crops like wheat or corn; they just take a while longer to grow back. Forests are renewable, but they are not crops. Crops are monocultures. Forests are evolving metacommunities. The complex cyclings of nutrients and energy that sustain them are still far from well understood. Nor do we have a clear idea yet of how the different stages of woodland growth should be balanced to promote maximum biological diversity and abundance. Until we do I can only suggest that we should be sure to leave a fair amount of maturity in our forests Overmaturity, if someone wants to use that slippery euthanasia salesman's word. Downright funky, overgrown antiquity. The kind that harbors molds and slugs and cathedral-size conifers with light filtering down from their crowns so high above through crystal snow and green needles, as if through the stained glass windows of medieval times whose colors no one knows how to make anymore.

Back and forth between the cutover North Fork property and the cathedral island laced the network of hoof and paw trails. In the sky arced a bridge of birds: mixed brigades of mountain chickadees, black-capped chickadees, and red-breasted nut-

COUGAR, MONTANA, NOVEMBER 1987

BOHEMIAN WAXWINGS, YELLOWSTONE NATIONAL PARK, WYOMING, NOVEMBER 1989

hatches in the lower branches. Pronouncements of ravens. A Steller's jay, mimicking the cry of a hawk. Pine grosbeaks and red crossbills swarming from treetop to treetop, ransacking cones for seeds. While American dippers, or ouzels, walked under the water's surface in search of caddis fly nymphs and other aquatic insect larvae.

On the far side of the island washed the rest of the river, and across that began Glacier National Park. Two other sides of the homestead were bordered by national forest acreage. Roughly half of the whole North Fork valley lies within Glacier National Park. The great majority of the other half is, like the land adjoining the homestead, state or national forest. Most of the wild creatures that belonged here were still here. I was seeing the things around me that I love to see, and, because of them, thinking about the sort of things that I like to think about. You can guess by the way I'm writing this that we were about to go back and tell our used car/used land man we were ready to deal. Poet Gary Snyder once said that you probably shouldn't live anywhere you wouldn't want to camp. I would camp here.

So we signed the papers, and as spring arrived jammed some belongings into the little tar-paper shack and started settling in. We hung a hummingbird feeder from a spruce in front of the shack. The thing was quickly populated by so many of these bumblebee birds—black-chinned, rufous, and calliope—that they spent more time fighting for a perch on its plastic flowers than feeding. During their aerial battles a surprising number of those dodging an aggressor tried to fly through the doorway of the shack. The main door was open. The screen door was not. In their dazzling hurry they didn't notice. The first thing we usually had to do upon returning from a walkabout was open the screen and push out frantically humming birds stuck by their bills in the mesh.

Among our shack's earlier occupants, we heard, were a couple of desperados who had shot up a bank, killed a clerk, and fled up the North Fork road, hoping to become lost to the world. As it turns out something of that sort happens every so often up this valley, with its road running fifty-some miles from the nearest Montana town and then on across the Canadian border into equally remote territory. Another occupant of the shack was a cougar, the previous owner told us. Actually, he said it was hiding underneath the shack while he and his buddies were staying there and spending the days hunting lions.

The first cat we saw at the place was an unwanted tabby that someone had dropped off along the road, thinking that it would at least have a fighting chance for survival. Something of that sort happens a little too often up this way as well. Apparently, the cat had spent a good deal of time on its own before it chanced upon the shack our first winter there, for it was as wary as any of the wild residents and probably leaner. We left it food on top of a stump and spent a long time sitting nearby on the front step, trying to ease its fears enough so that it would accept a touch. Then came the night that it ventured indoors and finally allowed itself to be held and stroked. It was the night of a January thaw, full of hissing wind and the scraping of tree against tree. After midnight I slipped off into troubled dreams, and the cat went

Bohemian waxwings (Bombycilla garrulus) are nomads, roaming mixed forests of the West and North in large flocks, searching for berries and other fruits along with insects, tree sap, and flowers. Their wanderings often lead them into suburban areas, where the flocks surge from yard to yard ransacking ornamental trees and shrubs such as mountain ash, hawthorn, and pyracantha for their berries. The gregarious birds often nest close together, but they neither nest nor winter in the same area from one year to the next. Instead they seem to go where the best berry crops appear—true vagrants, true bohemians. The waxwing part of their name refers to the waxy red substance coating the tips of their secondary feathers. First- and second-year birds have little or none, and it may be that the wax is a signal of age and social status. Older birds prefer to mate with one another, and they enjoy greater nesting success than younger, less experienced, subordinate pairs. Overall the Bohemian waxwing's plumage is fawn-colored and exceptionally soft and filmy. The crest on the head is another signal of age, as it is most prominent in fully grown adults.

145

Moose (Alces alces) roam boreal, or northern woodland, habitats throughout the northern hemisphere. Hanging from the throat area of both sexes, and especially conspicuous in the male, is a fold of flesh and hair known as the dewlap, or "bell." Its function is not well understood. The protuberance may simply add to the apparent size of an animal's profile during broadside displays in which individuals use body language to speak of their social rank. The two bulls depicted in this fall scene have come together to test one another's dominance during the rut. Moose seek out the rich aquatic vegetation of ponds and marshes through the warm months. They are said to be able to swim fast enough to match the pace of humans paddling a canoe. At times they submerge completely to feed, taking pondweed and lily stalks from as much as eighteen feet below the surface. As plant growth comes to an end in the fall they shift to browsing wetland shrubs, such as willow and dogwood. Moose are more solitary than most other members of the deer family, but they sometimes band together during winter, and the combined activity of their big hoofs keeps travel routes open through deep snow.

back outside. There, with its guard down, it was surprised by a mountain lion. Awakened by fierce squalling on the front porch, we pushed open the door to see the big cat a few feet away, looking up at us with the little cat broken in its mouth.

Cougars ordinarily show a healthy fear of things human. Possibly our lion didn't know much about people yet. More likely it knew but didn't much give a damn. This had been an easy winter with little snow, meaning that the hoofed animals were staying strong and fleet. It had therefore been a harder winter than usual for some of the predators. My guess is that this cougar was one of those, down on its luck, reduced to scrounging for easy pickings around cabins: dog food, dogs, cat food, cats . . . whatever. We now know that's one more thing the North Fork sees its share of: front-porch lions in the dead of winter. Their presence makes midnight trips to the outhouse more challenging than midnight trips to the outhouse really need to be. Yet while we found the big cat's tracks close by in the shallow snow for several more days, we never again saw the animal itself.

After spring break-up sent the ice from a second winter sluicing downstream we were ready to build a larger cabin. For logs we went to a neighbor's property two miles north and hauled back lodgepole pines killed by an outbreak of pine bark beetles. I don't remember the cabin-building as hard work. I just remember always seeming to have my arms full of something during the height of the mosquito season. Yet those were the weeks of serviceberry blossoms along every trail, followed by the time of wild roses. And I remember walking home along the track to the cabin at night after a supply run to town, sensing bushes in the dark as clumps of perfume, listening to the owls' chant and the river's thrum and, suddenly, the crashing of large bodies through the brush. Moose and elk mostly; bears sometimes. Anonymous bulks. By their grace we passed on.

The same blind encounters took place during the daytime and dusk when we wandered the thickets around the beaver dams. As the mergansers and goldeneyes emerged from their nests among the reeds of the largest pond with new broods lined out in their wake, the mothers appeared so nervous that the time had come for us to quit canoeing there for a while and let them pass on. Give and take.

We planted fruit trees within a lodgepole fence. Moose busted through the fence and ate the apple saplings. Deer jumped over the fence to try out some exotic apricot tree that the catalog promised would put out fruit in northern Siberia, but that was only getting smaller each month in the North Fork. We wrapped the last cherry saplings in burlap and chicken wire to protect them from cold and various members of the deer family. White-footed deer mice clambered up the wire and girdled every one. More give, more take: black bears left paw prints on the new cabin's windows on their way to the garden compost pile, which they demolished. We decided that we did not need any more compost. I won't bother to chronicle what happened to the garden.

In some heavily logged sections of the property we planted ponderosa pine seedlings, scattering them among the stumps and natural regrowth of shrubs. The deer

MOOSE, WYOMING, NOVEMBER 1989

MOUNTAIN GOATS, GLACIER NATIONAL PARK, MONTANA, JULY 1989

found every single one of those too. Why shouldn't they? You're welcome. They also took the sprouting grass and wildflowers in the meadow around the cabin, which gave us the pleasure of their company.

There comes a time between winter's end and early summer when the wild hoofed animals react much less strongly than usual to the presence of humans. For reasons no one has really explained they behave almost as if they were partially tame. During this generous season of detente we had deer out every window. We grew used to heads lifting up from the grass close by to watch us as we moved about outside. Ears would swivel briefly as we spoke to the deer in the soft sing-song that people find natural to use when trying to reassure animals. Then the heads would return to grazing, for the deer were growing steadily more used to us as well.

Around the beginning of June the first whitetails to be shed of their old winter hair took on sleek new coats the color of the valley's Indian paintbrush and cinnamon teal. At just about the same time some of the does would vanish. When they returned after a week or two, spotted fawns followed at their heels, looking us over.

It would not have been hard to have bears out the cabin window, too, as we discovered with our compost pile. Other folks up and down the valley learned the same lesson by leaving out dog food, garbage, smoked fish, hides, livestock in ripe-smelling pens, and the like. In spring we had to be especially thoughtful about what scents issued from our living quarters, for in addition to the black bears with year-round home ranges in the area, grizzlies were frequenting the bottomlands.

A friend of mine trains black bears and grizzlies for the entertainment industry. He knows as well as anyone how smart these omnivores are. His thirteen-hundred-pound Kodiak performs upon command any one of at least forty-five different behaviors—a versatile actor. Reflecting our dual perception of this beast, he is sometimes cast as the big bear buddy and the rest of the time plays the godawful monster role. What's your fancy? Should he dance with the mountain man or rear up like a thunderhead and turn the sucker into molehills? Wave hello or limp away into the sunset, licking his wounds? This bear, says my friend, picked up a number of the tricks in its repertoire on the very first try.

If a bear is lured to, say, your storage shed by a nice ripe smell, breaks in, and is rewarded with a snack, you may call yourself a bear trainer too. You have successfully taught the animal to associate easy-to-get food with human habitation. Unfortunately in the next scene, a frightened landowner shoots the bear. No, wait. Let's try this: the game department is called in to trap and remove it instead. When a trapped bear is released within a hundred or even two hundred miles of its original range, it is likely to find its way home and resume raiding. Or else, as when it is released farther afield, it finds its way to other human dwellings and takes up raiding there. *Then* the landowner shoots it.

Except in the case of the Geifer Grizz. Depending upon how you view things, this animal was either one bad outlaw or some sort of self-styled freedom fighter bent upon reminding us of who owned the land first. He first came to people's attention

The mountain goat (Oreamnos americanus) dwells in higher, steeper terrain than any other hoofed animal on the continent. It is not a true goat but the sole North American representative of the rupicaprid group, sometimes referred to as goat-antelopes, whose other members inhabit Eurasia. Like the mountain goat, they carry fairly short, sharp horns that are very similar in both sexes. Born in late May or early June, young mountain goats, called kids, are closely attended by their mothers, known as nannies. The nannies position themselves downhill from the youngsters in order to keep them from tumbling off the sheer cliff sides. After a week or so of seclusion nannies and their newborn kids rejoin herds on the mountainside. The kids soon seek out others their age for play. Their gambols are often juvenile versions of adult fighting patterns, which take the form of head-to-tail circling with each animal trying to hook the flank of its opponent with its horns. Kids also have play versions of adult courtship sequences, as seen here. Mountain goats usually remain on or close to the rock walls that keep them safe from most predators other than eagles, which snatch an occasional youngster. During summer, however, the goats make frequent forays from the cliffs to graze in lush alpine meadows. When a mountain goat band encounters a snowbank during such travels, the entire group is likely to erupt in a frenzy of play, with juveniles and adults alike leaping, whirling, and sliding down the sun-softened snowfield.

149

when he began trashing cabins in a new subdivision that sprang up within his home range. Game authorities captured him, punched metal tags through his ears for future identification, and turned him loose in a distant forest. He returned and took up cabin-wrecking where he had left off. He was caught again and released in a distant stretch of the North Fork, this time wearing a radio collar so that biologists could monitor his movements and dispatch him if he caused further trouble. The bear won his notoriety by going on to clobber some forty or fifty more cabins scattered through the valley.

He concentrated his efforts upon the bottomlands, swinging up and down the riverway, back and forth between the homesteads and vacation houses and wherever it was that he holed up in the mountains between raids. And he did this while pursued day and night by biologists and wardens with radio receivers and orders for an immediate execution. By the time his tale really got rolling he was also being trailed by special government hunters flown in from out of state. They were joined by God knows how many locals with CB radios and gun racks in their pickups, maybe some poison in their pocket, a grudge against bears, or a yen for fame as the man who nailed the one many had taken to calling "Mr. Geefer Goddamn Grizz."

Nobody nailed him, and the longer this lopsided contest went on, the more the bear's aura of canniness grew. He hit cabins to the north and south of us, but he left ours alone. Not because we did anything right; we were merely lucky. By then the Geifer knew all about what could be found inside cabins, whether you had any temptations lying around outside or not. Pretty soon, as cabin after cabin continued to get hit, a serious question arose as to who controlled the woods and the brushy places, who had dominion over the North Fork at night. Rumors that someone had gunned him down made the rounds several times. It always turned out to be the wrong bear. Then came the news that the Geifer Grizz was holed up in a cabin to the north, maybe making his final stand. Trucks and shooters surrounded the place and burst in. A radio collar lay on the floor amid the ruins of bedding and groceries. The bear that had worked it loose at last was off and running again. Even the grizz-haters had to admit it: this was some bear.

He trashed a few more cabins; then, like the human outlaws on the run up the North Fork before him, he headed for the Canadian line. Unlike most of them, he made it. Then he slept, far from any cabin. The following spring he passed the days feeding peacefully in a British Columbia meadow, his agenda in the North Fork complete for a while. The reason we know this is that an American hunter with a Canadian guide shot him there, understanding nothing about which bear this was or how he had lived. He reported the ear tags on the carcass. An early photograph of the Geifer Grizzly hangs framed on the log wall of the Northern Lights Saloon, next to the one store in the North Fork. A few of us still toast his memory there now and then. A couple of folks keep ashtrays made from a plaster cast of his pawprint. Other than that his story is over.

We tried to make sure that the spring grizzlies passing through our land found

NORTHERN GOSHAWK, OLYMPIC
NATIONAL PARK, WASHINGTON, APRIL 1989

only what they had been coming after for years: the earliest horsetail rushes, the tenderest shoots of cow parsnip, the lushest meadows of sprouting grass. They couldn't have done much better at our dinner table inside; some grasses contain about as much protein as cheese when they green up. On the island grizz dug up the roots of *Hedysarum*, a vetchlike legume rich in both protein and starch. Where this favorite food grew, the bears, somewhat like beavers, transformed the environment, cratering the gravelly floodplain beneath the cottonwoods until portions of it looked tilled by heavy machinery, like the alpine meadows roughed up by grizz excavating the bulbs of glacier lilies and spring beauties.

Across the river in the park we came upon a series of moist meadows during spring morning hikes. Islands of sunlight and tender unfurlings surrounded by dense lodgepole and leftover snow, these openings drew animals from miles around. In a single meadow we would often see nearly all the North Fork's common big species together.

The deer, elk, and moose were there, keeping only a casual eye on the grazing bears, the way African antelope do with nearby lions when it is clear from the cats' posture that they are not on the hunt. Ground squirrels grazed by the moving hoofs. Sometimes solitary coyotes waiting by a hole for a ground squirrel to pop up found knots of deer coming over to join them. The deer would mill and buck around the jackal-size dog and make sudden feints toward it until the coyote left, looking over its shoulder at the rowdies that had screwed up its chances of surprising any squirrels. Was it only a month ago that coyote packs harried deer through the crusted snowpack?

One meadow morning I came upon a pair of coyotes prancing around a grizzly. They took turns dashing in close enough to draw half-hearted charges from the bear, then raced away in tight circles. Since there was no disputed carcass at the center of this scene, I don't know what the coyotes' motives were. Entertainment, is my best guess. Spring chemistry makes us all a little strange and sassy at times. We act as if we were leading charmed lives. But then if such a thing as spring can arise from the frozen mud remains of a Rocky Mountain winter, maybe, in fact, we are.

Without planning to, I developed a habit of hiking to at least one meadow practically every morning. I told myself that it was mainly to learn more about grizzlies as a naturalist. It would be truer to say that I just wanted to watch the things. And I suppose it was not even so much to watch the great bears themselves as to watch everything around me while feeling as alert and alive as grizz make me feel when they are somewhere close.

I usually started off in the twilight before dawn, following a route that kept me near climbable trees. Except on the frostiest mornings, I went barefoot to keep my noise down. My toes thought it was a splendid idea after a winter in heavy boots and seldom snapped a twig. At that hour of the morning the air was generally calm. Any wind would be reflected in the long black threads of lichen draped from the lodgepole's branches, so light they would sail sideways on a breath. As soon as they started

WHITE-TAILED DEER SKULL, NEBRASKA, MAY 1986

GLACIER BEAR, GLACIER BAY,
ALASKA, JUNE 1986

moving I left so that my man-stench wouldn't upset the bears. The point was to be able to observe the animals doing exactly what they would have been doing if I were not there. I knew from tracks around my home that grizz had gone about their business within scent, sound, and, occasionally, sight of us without disturbing our day. Give and take.

Some of the black bears of the meadows were actually yellow or brown. One of the grizzlies was charcoal black. Seeing the two species in the same field of grass at one time was a springtime anomaly on the order of deer chasing coyotes. At other times grizzlies may kill and eat black bears they encounter within their home range. Favoring relatively open habitats, grizzlies reinforce the black bear's role as more of a creature of the forests, where it has the advantage of being able to escape up a tree. A grizzly's claws, specialized for digging, become too long and straight in the adult to support the animal's weight on a tree trunk. (It is not altogether true that big grizz can't climb trees, though. Given stout branches that begin low enough to the ground, the great bear is capable of hauling itself up to a considerable height pawhold by pawhold—worth keeping in mind in grizzly country.)

Odd: I'd creep in toward a meadow, pumped tight with adrenaline, coiling to jump whenever a deer burst from behind a shrub, grabbing tree bark when a ruffed grouse boomed out its mating call, which sounds like a two-cycle generator suddenly starting up. Finally, peeking out from behind the last tree, I might find myself looking at the biggest and most powerful bear yet. The Grizz of Grizz. Which would proceed to munch its grassy pasture for a solid hour without once lifting its head to peer over a shoulder or test the air, displaying all the untamed ferocity of a dairy cow. Yet that was a revelation in its own right—to be in the presence of a wild creature that didn't have to look around itself if it didn't want to. Because it was afraid of nothing in its world—a live definition of indomitable. The next visit, if it was in late May or early June, might turn up a courting pair whose growls, chases, and shiver-quick sparrings overwhelmed the green clearing. Karen was luckier than I. She saw a pair advance one morning from a feisty courtship to mating and then to an afterglow of side-by-side companionship in the early light.

By eight o'clock on a typical morning, we would be back home. The sun would just be beginning to heat up the bottomlands. Already we would have had a good, full day. Whatever else happened was a bonus. And we experienced it while still in that open-eared, roving-eyed, up-on-your-toes state awakened by bear meadow mornings. It is not a jittery feeling, this moment-by-moment keenness. It is simply a different pitch of existence more closely matched to wildness. After a while it is more like bathing in the currents of the natural world. Peaceful. Cleansing. Part of the process of settling into a place, the giving and the taking, that can continue without limit.

If someone asks me, then, what good is a grizzly, I would answer: It has the power to smash every illusion that keeps you separate from nature. It teaches attentiveness and humility. In the end it instructs in communion.

A glacier bear, also known as the blue bear, nibbles the tender spring leaves of an alder bush. Considered a rare color phase of the black bear (Ursus americanus), it is found in Alaska's Glacier Bay National Park region. Its frost-colored hairs give it a superficial resemblance to the grizzly bear (Ursus arctos horribilis), with its characteristic silver-tipped fur. Black and grizzly bear ranges overlap throughout much of the North and portions of the West, and a considerable amount of confusion exists in identifying the two species, because both come in a wide assortment of colors and sizes. Whatever its hue, a black bear is characterized by a fairly smooth back and short, strongly curved claws that enable it to readily hook into bark and climb trees. Grizzlies, by contrast, have a pronounced muscular hump at the shoulder, a dished-looking face, and relatively straight claws that are up to four or five inches long—ideal for digging up roots and burrowing rodents but no longer effective for tree-climbing once the animal reaches adult size. Another unique color phase of the black bear is the Kermode's bear of interior British Columbia. It is not black at all but, rather, almost solid white.

155

A great blue heron flies back to its rookery on an island a short distance upriver. I hear the familiar call, the deep grawking sounds that seem carried by strange winds from a far earlier epoch. Without turning around I can see in my mind the slow cadence of six-foot-long wings not far above the cottonwoods, the long trailing legs, the red-legged frogs and sculpins in its throat, destined for the nest, the cuneiform patterns of the toe prints in mud along the channel's shore. A beaver slaps the water with its tail; I can't see the channel, but I can tell from the sun on the leaves around me what color the water's rippling surface will be. Its spectrum under different skies in different seasons is inside me now, like the cast of leaves in different degrees of wind.

When a grizzly moves, its silver-tipped fur shimmers and changes color, as if arcs of power were rippling off it. I do not think I would know the heron, the beaver, or even the trembling leaf as I do if not for the grizzlies somewhere out there moving between them, lending each of us a measure of that power.

Back in the cabin I work the pump handle by the sink, and stonefly larvae come pouring out into my drinking glass. There are around forty different species of them in the North Fork River, whose flow continues below the riverbed through the glacial gravel deposits. Some stonefly nymphs have been found passing part of their lives at least two hundred feet underground. We dig holes three feet down, which we will fill with concrete in a week or so, making footings for a building. Each morning until then we remove the long-toed salamanders and red-backed voles that fell in during nighttime errands otherwise hidden from our view, like stoneflies deep in the magical earth.

Winter mornings, we feed the gray jays and whistle-talk with them a while, then watch them pack their groceries back to caches in trees. The sticky saliva with which they coat such stored food may inhibit the growth of bacteria. Sometimes they hang out with Clark's nutcrackers, another bold, conversational member of the jay family. Nutcrackers occasionally ride around on the backs of ungulates on winter ranges, waiting for the big animals to paw through the snow and uncover seeds. In return for the lift they pick off wood ticks wandering through the ungulates' fur. They also serve as an early warning system, alerting fellow birds and feeding ungulates alike with an alarm call when they spot intruders. In other words we aren't the only mammals listening to what these birds have to say.

After jays and breakfast we walk or ski to see what the day holds by way of fresh tracks. On a frozen morning more than a decade ago I intersected a set of prints entirely new to our home range. They read wolf. Canis lupus. Once as abundant and widespread as early humans throughout North America—and the rest of the northern hemisphere—wolves were almost completely eradicated south of Canada by early in this century. They have since reestablished a population of about thirteen hundred in the northern Great Lakes region. Just one other part of the United States outside Alaska has a known breeding group today. That is the North Fork of the Flathead, which already harbors one of the Lower 48's best surviving grizzly popula-

ALASKAN BROWN BEARS, ALASKA, JULY 1988

CANADA GEESE, SEATTLE, WASHINGTON, MARCH 1989

tions. (Red wolves, *Canis rufus*, native to America's Southeast, were entirely gone from the wild until the last couple of years, when a few survivors bred in captivity were released in North and South Carolina wildlife refuges.)

To say that wolves have established themselves in the North Fork sounds too assured. The reality is this: in 1978, the year those tracks cut the corner of our property, a single black wolf was seen just across the border in British Columbia. At first hardly anyone paid much attention. Although wolves were scarce throughout that southern region of Canada, a few small packs still live in the spine of the Rockies toward Kootenay, Yoho, and Banff national parks, which lie about a hundred miles north. And wolves are long-legged travelers. So it was not really unexpected when some drifted across the border. They usually came alone, like this one, and they never seemed to stay long. Or if they did, they never seemed to live long. Most of the sightings of wolves in Montana over the decades involved a wolf shot, snared, or poisoned.

The black wolf hung around the North Fork border for another year, then dropped out of sight just as a research project to study a possible wolf recovery got underway. Come spring, however, the biologists captured a gray, eighty-pound female in the same area. They gave her a Kootenay Indian name—Kishinena—after the bright tributary draining from British Columbia through the northwest tip of Glacier National Park, and they began following her with the help of a radio collar.

Kishinena moved with the game, at times traveling deeper into Canada toward the North Fork headwaters. She ate moose, beavers, snowshoe hares, ground squirrels, mice, voles, and spruce grouse. That was how the sign read. She might have eaten elk, mule deer, and whitetails too. She scavenged, running down the scent of leftover meat, as often as she killed. And in summertime she also picked berries. She avoided human footprints and ski trails, reversing direction when she happened upon them. In the next fifteen months she visited Montana once, near Kishinena Creek. As far as anyone knew, she was always alone.

Those were the raw data. To the handful of us locals who had taken an interest in her as a kind of shadow neighbor, the data didn't seem to make her all that much more real. A wolf's intelligence, like our dogs' and our own, is essentially social. The wolf survives best in packs because the hoofed prey it depends upon are smart, sensitive, and socially alert as well—and often bigger, faster, and stronger than a single wolf. What was it really like, then, to be a lone, eighty-pound female trying to keep alive in our valley? How did it feel in the gut? In the mind? What did it mean to have a song, an old tune, going round in her head, but never a chorus? What were her chances here? All we had to go on was this skin-and-bones outline.

Researchers followed Kishinena through another winter. Her tracks remained a solitary line even when blood on the snow indicated that Kishinena was in heat. She was already middle-aged. I held little hope that she would ever see offspring. Then another winter, another breeding season alone. Always alone. And always, there were men visiting these woods who plumb hated wolves, or thought they were supposed

Canada geese (Branta canadensis) build their nests atop matted cattails and bulrushes, muskrat and beaver houses, haystacks and houses, and now and again in tall trees. Not surprisingly, they readily accept the artificial nest platforms built at many refuges. The female does the nest-building and incubates the four to ten eggs while the male, or gander, stands guard close by. When the eggs hatch after about a month, both parents lead the young off to a rearing area, which may be some distance away. Thereafter, both parents attend the young as they travel, often with the gander leading and the female bringing up the rear. When alarmed, the goslings dive, and the male performs a display to distract the predator. By the time the goslings are several weeks old the parents undergo their postnuptial molt, becoming as flightless as their offspring. The nonbreeding segment of the population—juveniles, adults that failed to win mates, and those that lost their broods—gathers and undertakes what is known as a molt migration. They leave the breeding ground, usually headed north, and travel hundreds or even thousands of miles away to a particular molting ground. Geese from the Great Basin, for example, are known to have traveled nearly to Hudson Bay for the molt period. Such summer movements reduce competition for the parents and their growing goslings back on the breeding grounds.

159

GRAY WOLF YOUNG, ALASKA, JULY 1985

to. Sure enough, as in the heyday of the Geifer Grizzly, rumors filtered through the valley that she had been done in. Shoot, shovel, and shut up. The usual deal.

Then the black wolf reappeared. In the moist, packed snow of spring details of the paws became clear. One foot of the black wolf was missing a toe, most likely left in someone's steel-jawed trap. This told us something we already knew: the black wolf was a survivor. Together, his tracks and the female's wound through the country. Later in the spring, Kishinena bore seven pups in a den just within British Columbia. They grew up, most of them, and became a functional group operating on both sides of the border. Called the Magic Pack—partly for its ability to suddenly vanish from human ken for long periods and then materialize just as unexpectedly, and partly for the fact that it existed at all—it soon began denning in Glacier.

From this beginning the little group should have expanded into a larger one, then divided into several different groups with various leaders, or alpha wolves. It did just that, but more slowly than anticipated. Members were shot from new logging roads pushed into the once-remote corner of southeastern British Columbia. Some were trapped. Still others dispersed to unknown countrysides. In order to protect habitat critical to the wolf's recovery on the United States side from harmful developments, it was necessary to establish that there was, in fact, a recovering wolf pack there. Yet money for the research project ran out. A solitary scientist named Diane Boyd kept the tracking work alive, often funding it out of her own pocket. As Kishinena had for so long, and as the pack was doing now, she endured from day to day.

Then B.C. game managers opened an unlimited hunting and trapping season on the predators in the Canadian province's share of the North Fork. The pelts taken as a result included breeding females crucial to the future of the extended Magic Pack. One female managed to produce a litter of pups in Glacier recently, but they died under mysterious circumstances, and the pack returned to Canada for a while.

It has been a dozen years now since I first saw those wolf tracks near home. I have seen more since, and heard wolves howl from across the river. So they are around, still trailing signs and songs behind them. But I could not tell you where they are going, or when—or even if—they will be able to return as an integral part of the ecosystem.

I wish I knew. A fundamental issue revolves around wolves. Are we really out to conserve wildness? Or only the pieces that suit us? To the extent that we pick and choose pieces, wildlife communities will reveal that much more about the temporary goals of human communities and that much less about the holistic workings of nature. How, then, shall we ever understand creation?

I do not think it is possible to truly understand even one leg muscle of one elk in the absence of wolves. Not a single leap of a single deer, nor any traverse of any mountain goat across a winterbound cliff wall. The size and endurance of hoofed beasts on this continent; their speed, coordination, and quicksilver reactions; their social structure and communication abilities—wolves sang these things into their present form.

Anywhere from one to eleven pups may appear when a female gray wolf (Canis lupus) gives birth. Both parents, which mate for life, take part in the care and feeding of the young. Various other members of the pack often help as well. Adults returning to the den regurgitate food for the pups, a process perhaps stimulated by the pups themselves as they bite and tug at the corners of the adult's mouth. Wolves will change den sites if disturbed. Once the pups are more mobile the birth den is usually abandoned for less protected living quarters, known as rendezvous sites. From there the youngsters begin to explore their range a bit at a time, always under the tutelage and protection of adult pack members. As wolf pups tussle in play, they gain not only skill and coordination but also a knowledge of one another's strength and initiative, which will translate into social ranking within the pack as the animals mature. When populations become fairly dense in relation to prey, wolves naturally limit their numbers. Aggression increases within social groups. Fewer pups than usual are produced, and, of those that are born, fewer than usual live to maturity. Conversely, wolves compensate for heavy losses and low densities through increased birth rates and survival of young.

161

Throughout history owls have often been reviled as harbingers of doom, witches' companions, or at least chicken thieves, but perhaps no owl has been the subject of so many curses as the spotted owl (Strix occidentalis) is today. The reason: extensive clearcut logging throughout the dense conifer woodlands where this bird of prey lives—the Northwest and south along the Pacific coast—has reduced it to a seriously threatened species. A breeding pair of spotted owls may require up to forty-five hundred acres of mature, primary forest for their territory, which they remain in for life. Some people see such a tract as part of one of our most complex, least understood, and most rapidly vanishing ecosystems—primeval temperate rainforest. Others see timber worth tens of millions of dollars rotting away "unused," and out-of-work sawyers sport bumper stickers saying, Save a Logger, Eat a Spotted Owl. Spotted owls are neither very adaptable nor prolific to begin with. Pairs do not breed every year, and the survival of young to breeding age appears naturally low. Moreover, these owls have such thick plumage as an adaptation to their damp, shady environment that they have trouble shedding heat when exposed to even moderately high temperatures. Where they cannot readily find cool microclimates—as when logging has removed the canopy—survival rates may drop lower still. Whatever its own fate may prove to be, the spotted owl has become the symbol of the battle over the fate of our old-growth forests and all the other animals and plants that depend upon them.

Wolves were the major predator of large ungulates here for thousands of animal generations; omnipresent, efficient, relentlessly separating the fit from the less splendid. It was the creatures some people loathe that fashioned the creatures so many admire. As our chief competitors for meat, on the hoof or around fresh carcasses, and as the preeminent teachers of group hunting techniques, they surely fashioned early human society to some extent as well. In the North Fork the type of enlightened stewardship that would encourage the recovery of wolves would also assure future open space, natural diversity, and sensible resource development, values important for human society in modern times.

Some argue that wolves are more or less obsolete now—that there are enough human hunters afield to prevent overpopulation by prey animals and the starvation and disease epidemics that might follow. Maybe so. However, human hunters do not hunt in the fashion wolves do, and are nowhere near as selective of prey that lack speed, strength, or stamina. Therefore, they cannot create the same sort of elk—or antelope or bighorn sheep—that wolves can. Sooner or later those prey species will evolve along noticeably different lines, becoming something that embodies not wolves but the absence of wolves. Nature does not stand still. You cannot, says the wolf, save just the pieces. You have to save the process, or the pieces won't keep.

That's what good wolves are: they speak of origins and continuity. They instruct in the meaning of wholeness.

Calling wolves obsolete or unnecessary is the updated version of the frontier ethic that dismissed wolves as cruel, greedy, wasteful, and so on. It parallels the way the colonial view of primeval forests as trackless wastes evolved into the relatively sophisticated term "overmature." Moral judgments about nature leave me queasy, especially those presented in the guise of modern scientific management. They remain conclusions in search of facts. Science is precisely the opposite.

Failing to distinguish between the two is likely to seriously impoverish us over the long run, and not just in terms of natural resources. We risk squandering one of the greatest spiritual resources offered each person: the chance to comprehend the live world that shapes and sustains us and to find meaning in our place within it. We risk confusing our own direct experience of the kingdom with someone else's ideas of how nature should be, or what it ought to mean. Heavy stuff, that baggage of preconceived notions. It's the equivalent of trying to hold your head up to absorb a grand scene along the trail with a hopelessly overloaded pack slung on your shoulders.

Most people have moved away from the old agrarian-pastoralist moral order that viewed wild nature not only as unproductive but as threatening and pagan. Yet, interestingly, most people—including many who support conservation—still think of wild or untamed as synonymous with unpredictable. I think the opposite is true. Nature is the deep, ultimate predictability offered in this world. You can count on its honesty, bet your life on its processes; we all do at some level.

As with our perception of great bears, most of what we describe as unpredictable stems from a lack of familiarity with the lives at hand. In the North Fork, where we

162

SPOTTED OWL IN OLD-GROWTH FOREST, WASHINGTON, JUNE 1989

Mallards (Anas platyrhynchos), such as the hen and three drakes shown here, are among the largest of the dabbling ducks. In ponds they tip up their tails and submerge the fronts of their bodies to feed on both soft submerged vegetation and insects and molluscs; nesting females eat twice the amount of animal protein that males and nonlaying females do. Along the shores they graze on grasses and sedges. And they make daily flights to harvest in-season grains, fruits, and nuts from surrounding areas. (Mallards have even been seen feeding on the remains of salmon washed up along the shore at the end of a spawning run.) Such a generalized, adaptable foraging strategy has helped make mallards the most widespread and abundant ducks across most of the continent. For that matter, they are probably the most common ducks in the entire northern hemisphere. Mallards captured and bred in ancient Mesopotamia or possibly China gave rise to almost all the familiar breeds of domestic ducks. The mating of wild mallards with domestic breeds in many rural areas and parks today continues to produce all manner of hybrids. Mallards also hybridize with the closely related American black duck (Anas rubripes).

had far more animals than people for neighbors, we could hardly help but relate to the creatures and their daily and seasonal activities as some of the most familiar, constant things in our lives. Nature was no longer a separate world. It was not a spectacle we went to see now and again, not our choice of recreation, not an adjunct to our existence. It was our existence. It encompassed and overwhelmed. Immersed in its rhythms, voices, unfoldings, wheelings, prowlings, blossomings, dyings, we regained some of our species's old trust with wildness.

Trust, along with a solid sense of belonging, is exactly what's missing from the modern urban social contract. City life offers a heady mix of excitement, congestion, material comfort, pollutants, human-made beauty, crime, fast-changing technologies, and even more fleeting social styles. *That* is unpredictable. Spending time in wild places is not particularly risky if you know what you are doing: living without running water or electricity, as we did in the North Fork, is not a hardship. Living without being able to make sense of your surroundings—without being sure of their meaning, fending off the malaise of insecurity, alienation, and stress so characteristic of our psychologically fragmented century: *that* is hard, risky work.

Once you know a wild place well enough to carry on a continual conversation with it you discover how articulate nature can be. It is coherent and comprehensible, making eloquent sense without the double and triple layers of meaning that people have to wade through in conversing among themselves. Who am I? What does my life count for? To be able to turn and sweep a hand across a wild setting such as the North Fork, outlined by mountains and filled by free-living creatures, and say, "I am part of this" is enough of an answer for now.

I don't mean to slip into the romantic tradition in which whatever animals do is right and noble, while human actions are corrupted by lies and selfish desires. I might as well be ranting about savage wolverines slinking through stagnant forests. The nature-good/people-guilty syndrome that emerges from some nature writing may turn the old morality upside down, but it only reinforces the idea that the human sphere and the wild sphere are quite separate. And that rift is what sabotages clear conservation thinking. I'm after common ground.

It wouldn't be fair, either, to make it appear as if all we did around our home was stroll hither and yon in a state of rhapsody—another romantic nature writing tradition. The truth is that Karen and I devoted big chunks of time to other important things: drinking coffee at neighbors' cabins, playing volleyball at the Northern Lights Saloon or hockey on the frozen river, changing diapers, and the like. There were also weathered-in times when we just plain sat in our little cabin among the piney woods, bored witless.

Another thing Karen and I did was worry a lot. The more we settled into our North Fork way of life over the years, the more things appeared to threaten it. We would look over our shoulder from a scene that seemed just right, and a proposal for a massive open-pit coal mine, coal-fired power plant, and major townsite just across the Canadian line would rear up and snarl at us. Then it was a proposal to pave the nar-

MALLARDS, WASHINGTON, MARCH 1989

BLACK-TAILED DEER, OLYMPIC NATIONAL FOREST, WASHINGTON, APRIL 1989

row dirt road, which would have accelerated subdivision and commercial development throughout the valley. Then logging plans for a roadless portion of prime grizzly habitat. Then several years in a row of bombing—setting off seismic charges to map the rocks' potential for oil. Helicopters roamed along the Whitefish Range day after day, delivering dynamite to be exploded every two hundred feet. And our two children would come running to us across the yard crying, asking, "Mom, Dad, what was that?" Why, it's the sound of America freeing itself from foreign oil, kids. It's our way of supporting afternoon-long rush hours in Los Angeles. What were we supposed to say?

Then more poorly conceived logging. Then proposals for oil and gas drilling. Like the coal mine and road paving, they were deflected. Then, as I began writing this book, a drilling rig went in two miles away. They say there is a chance of a gas blowout with sulfide fumes that could kill residents within that radius. And people from out of state still ask us: Isn't it a little dangerous living way out in the woods with bears and all? Kind of unpredictable? If the drillers find major reserves, refineries and pipelines would follow. So would housing for workers, stores, and the rest of the infrastructure that could transform the valley and its quality of life for people and animals alike.

Which is what we had worried about all along. In settling into the right home, as with marrying or having children, you discover capacities for love within yourself that you did not know existed before. At the same time you are almost afraid to love anything so much, knowing that if it were to be taken away, the loss might destroy you. I always felt a fool or a bit of a coward for holding back a little in my love for the North Fork because of my fears for its future. Now I think perhaps it was the best thing to do, or I might have had my heart broken along the way.

As it turned out we stopped living there year-round three years ago, when our children came of school age. We live about forty miles downstream during the school year now, returning to North Fork life some weekends and then throughout each summer. It is still the place I think of as home. I imagine we will return again for good when the children take up their own lives as young adults. I imagine myself in a place where wildness always awaits—knowing full well that it may not be able to wait very long.

The mule deer (Odocoileus hemionus) is distributed throughout western North America in a variety of forms. In the coastal region of the Pacific Northwest lives the subspecies known as the Columbian black-tailed deer (Odocoileus hemionus columbianus). Mature bucks weigh 110 to 250 pounds; does average 100 pounds—less than two-thirds as much as typical mule deer bucks and does. The tail is solid black; a typical mule deer tail is black only at the tip. In addition to being smaller and darker than other mule deer, black-tailed deer are somewhat more nocturnal. They also form smaller social groups, possibly because they occupy thicker, more heavily timbered habitat such as the coastal rainforest depicted here.

167

NORTHERN GANNETS, CAPE ST. MARY'S, NEWFOUNDLAND, JULY 1989

HARBOR SEAL, MONTEREY PENINSULA, CALIFORNIA, SEPTEMBER 1989

HUMPBACK WHALE, SOUTHEAST ALASKA, AUGUST 1989

CHAPTER EIGHT

New Found Land

AT THE EASTERNMOST EDGE of Canada, separated from the mainland by the Gulf of St. Lawrence, stands the big Atlantic isle known as Newfoundland. Its easternmost edge is the Avalon Peninsula, and that is as far as the continent stretches. Beyond Avalon's shores it is all and always the sea.

A cold sea. The Labrador current sweeping past the coast is formed by the union of waters out of Hudson Bay and the Davis Strait off Greenland. During spring break-up, rafts of pack ice flow south in the stream's grip. Fishermen call the softening chunks that wash by Avalon "slob ice." Sometimes villagers there awaken in midsummer to find a crystal mountain risen just beyond the edge of the flowering land. This vision—this manifestation of opal light—is a giant iceberg sailing slowly past on a journey begun perhaps two years earlier when it calved from an arctic glacier.

Once in a while a polar bear arrives with the ice and disembarks to explore the countryside. One showed up in Newfoundland's capital city, St. John's. If I were a white bear wandering into a world of crowded intersections and convenience stores, I might see it as something akin to the noisy breeding colonies of seals or seabirds that generate traffic elsewhere along the coast. What the bear itself made of the place, no one knows. The authorities were called in, and they terminated the sea hunter's long voyage.

Settlers reached the Avalon Peninsula from various parts of the British Isles, which actually lie farther north in the Atlantic than Newfoundland but among warmer currents. The newcomers fished, and they raised a few sheep along the coast, with its grassy hills and forests of balsam fir and spruce. But the peninsula's interior remained largely impermeable to civilization.

Ice Age glaciers gouged Newfoundland hard. The soils that have developed atop the scratched rock since then are thin. They also tend to be acidic, poorly drained, and lacking in nutrients. Such conditions produced the peatlands that now cover some 25 percent of the province—bogs, fens, sphagnum marshes, moors, heaths, call them what you will. Much of the interior of Avalon is a stony tundra barrens that seems to have dropped in from the true Arctic like an iceberg or polar bear. The locals just call it "the Country." What little human activity did mark the land here—tree-cutting and fires—only increased the size of the barrens.

Some eighty-eight thousand acres at the core of the Country were chosen as the Avalon Wilderness Reserve, Newfoundland's first protected wildland area. It is the heart of a range now used by nearly six thousand caribou.

Identifiable by their long whitish flippers, humpback whales (Megaptera novaeangliae) are very often seen breaching. Spectacular leaps take place during courtship, and it has been suggested that pairs may actually mate while rising together into the air. These whales are known for their elaborate, enchanting songs, and more recently for their use of bubble nets to round up fish schools while feeding. The baleen plates through which the mysticetes, or toothless whales, strain their catches of fish and krill are made of the same protein substance—keratin—that forms horns, hoofs, claws, and hair in land-based mammals.

171

At Delaware Bay, where between half a million and one and a half million shorebirds stop off for three to four weeks each spring, two ruddy turnstones (Arenaria interpres) join a crowd of red knots (Calidris canutus). The red knot was probably this continent's most abundant shorebird before nineteenth-century market hunting obliterated the majority of its population. The first nest of this large, tundra-breeding sandpiper species wasn't reported until 1909, when members of Peary's expedition found one on their way to the North Pole. In autumn the red knot leaves its arctic range and flies toward the opposite pole, wintering as far south as Tierra del Fuego, where many turnstones end up as well. This stop-off in Delaware Bay during their return toward the Arctic coincides with the arrival of huge numbers of horseshoe crabs. The crabs come to the bay to deposit their egg masses just beneath the surface on tidal flats, and the mixed shorebird flocks probing the mud find themselves with an almost unlimited supply of protein to fuel their northward travels. Ordinarily turnstones do exactly what their name implies, flipping over pebbles and stones to feed on marine invertebrates. Once on their nesting grounds they rely more upon tundra insects. Ruddy turnstones are also known to take berries in season, and to prey upon the eggs of other birds, notably terns.

Eurasia's reindeer, wild and tame, and caribou belong to the same species, *Rangifer tarandus*. North America has four subspecies in its arctic regions. These include the great migratory herds familiar to many people and the diminutive, snow white Peary's caribou, which hardly anyone knows, found on Ellsmere Island, Canada's northernmost reach in the polar sea. The caribou of Avalon belong to a fifth subspecies: woodland caribou. This is the largest of all, the darkest, and the least gregarious, living in small family bands. Like the woodland bison, it was plentiful in the boreal forest zone from one end of the continent to the other not so very long ago.

Caribou have an interesting outlook on risk. I've observed wolves, bears, and humans walk right up to within a few dozen yards of caribou groups. But then none of us has feet as large in proportion to body size as the caribou's wide-spreading hoofs. As a result none can race across spongy, hummocky peatland and soft snow as swiftly. Not quite, and that is the margin that counts. The caribou seem to know it. It is as if they sense just how much of a headstart they need for an escape and don't worry overmuch about danger beyond that point. In fact, caribou commonly take the initiative and walk over to check out a nearby human or predator.

Whatever the natural function of this personality trait, it wasn't very useful once Europeans arrived with their guns. It merely made the big northern deer foolproof targets. At the same time woodland caribou were beginning to lose vast swatches of their homeland. Unlike the Avalon herd, most woodland caribou did dwell in real woodlands, selecting the boggier taiga sections that offered lichens, moss, and sedge as forage. Before long these boreal forests were being mined for timber on a massive scale and cleared for agriculture. The peatlands amidst cutover stands dried out. Marshes were drained. Fires became more frequent.

While caribou were going homeless, white-tailed deer flourished as never before. They were already adapted to disturbance, in the sense that secondary, or successional, habitats created in the forest by such natural forces as flood, fire, or windstorms had long provided their chief food and shelter. As for the behavior required to survive close to human settlement, whitetails are one of the standards by which we define wariness. How can "alert as a deer" be improved upon? It is part of our store of living definitions. As far as caribou are concerned, however, an accumulation of whitetails is no blessing. They carry a parasitic roundworm that invades membranes of the nervous system. Transmitted to caribou, the disease proves far more lethal than to the whitetails themselves.

Beset on several fronts at once, woodland caribou soon became relatively uncommon in Canada. In the United States the animals vanished completely from the four New England states they had populated. By about 1940 the last were gone as well from their three native states in the Great Lakes region. Out West woodland caribou are known as mountain caribou. Like all the other kinds of caribou, they winter chiefly on lichen. But they depend upon the type that grows hanging from branches, the arboreal lichen most people describe as tree moss or old man's beard. Western caribou find it mainly in old-growth forests above forty-five hundred feet. By the

RUDDY TURNSTONES AND RED KNOTS, DELAWARE BAY, MAY 1989

HARBOR SEALS, VANCOUVER ISLAND, BRITISH COLUMBIA, MAY 1989

1950s the sole caribou herd south of Canada was made up of mountaineers roaming the Selkirk Range of Idaho and adjoining segments of Washington and Montana. As of 1980 barely thirty of those were still alive.

The following year a lone male, probably from southern British Columbia, wandered down Montana's Whitefish Range, past my cabin next to Glacier National Park. He was spotted licking salt with the cows at a neighbor's ranch. Mountain caribou used to be part of the Glacier National Park ecosystem. With less excessive road building and clearcut logging in the old-growth timber stands of the high country around the park, they could be part of the fabric again. Should be. Deserve to be. Surely we deserve to have them around.

I missed glimpsing the male that turned up at my neighbor's. But that winter a biologist and I tracked down eight adult members of the Selkirk herd and three young, the first offspring researchers had observed for some time. A project to bolster the Selkirk remnant with mountain caribou from British Columbia finally won official approval, and is underway today as I write. The largest single woodland caribou population on the continent at present is a herd of about nine thousand in the middle of Newfoundland. Next largest is the Avalon Peninsula herd, from which a number of animals were recently transplanted to Maine.

So you'll be going to the Country, will you? asked the people I spoke with in Trepassey on Avalon's southern shore. The Country runs down close to here, they said, and a lot of caribou come this way in the late spring and summer. First the stags, then the cows with their new calves. Mind you, you seldom heard of any around Trepassey until maybe a dozen years ago. But then forty years back, they had been shot down to where there were only a couple hundred caribou on the whole peninsula. Funny creatures. Some prefer the trees, or at least the tuckamoors, where clumps of dwarfed spruce grow dense as hedges. Some keep to the barrens all the time. Oh, you'll likely see some of those not too many miles out of town, as soon as you rise up onto the Country. Providing the weather doesn't turn sour like it did last night.

A Welsh colony was founded around Trepassey quite early. By 1620 it had already gone under. Trepassey means "the dead souls." I don't know whether or not that is because the area is so often swept into a limbo of fog and cold winds.

The day was a low gray thing with seagulls battering against its roof as Art Wolfe and I drove out of Trepassey, and when we reached the Country, it was streaming with mist. Still, we did find caribou almost at once: one band, two, another, a group of thirty or more behind them. These Avalon animals looked as arctic as their barrenland range, far whiter than any woodland caribou I had imagined. Although it was June, they hadn't yet shed their old winter coats. Some males had streaks of brown on their backs. The rest looked like clotted fog.

Most of the animals were following meandering streamcourses from pool to pond on their way toward the sea. Soil deposits were a little thicker along these drainage channels, enough to support plush green carpets of sedge. Plant growth in general was more advanced here near the coast than in the interior, which may be part of

The harbor seal (Phoca vitulina) is also called the common seal, for good reason. Its range is the widest of any seal species, and it is easily observed, as it spends quite a bit of time ashore on rocks of the intertidal zone. Along the Atlantic coast harbor seals occur from the Arctic to the Carolinas. Pacific populations extend from the Bering Sea to Baja California. They may vary their seasonal ranges locally, but are not really migratory. Five to six feet long and weighing 200 to 290 pounds, harbor seals belong to the family Phocidae, known as the earless seals. They do have ears but lack obvious external signs of them. Phocids are thought to be descended from primitive otterlike carnivores drawn to the bounty of the sea. Born ashore in May or June after a nine-month gestation period, harbor seal pups wear blue-gray fur above and whitish fur below, and are capable of swimming on their own as soon as the first tide comes in.

175

what draws the animals in this direction each spring. Another factor may be the strong seaside breezes that help keep down emerging insect hordes. Blackflies and mosquitoes both have aquatic larvae that thrive in the sodden peatlands. Under similar conditions in the arctic tundra mosquitoes alone can cost caribou a quart of blood or more per week. Then there are deer-nose botflies, *Cephenomyia*, which deposit their larvae in nasal passages, where the grubs wriggle around feeding on the sensitive tissues, driving the caribou half-crazy. Here is one predator caribou can't outrun, though I've seen them try, frantically. Adult *Cephenomyia*, one of the fastest insects known, have been timed flying at fifty miles per hour.

Art wanted to stalk upwind to reach some caribou a ways to the north and see what kind of images he could make of them drifting along in the fog. I threw on a daypack, saying I would meet him and his cameras on the road in a couple of hours, then started in the opposite direction along a stream. In no time I was out of view of all things man-made, just trekking between long, slow swells of land. The floating sensation I felt was not my imagination: each step I took was cushioned with the silvery lichen called caribou moss and hummocks of cottongrass sedge and pale laurel.

For the previous three months I had been in Africa. The last part of that trip involved trekking through the Congo Basin. Day after day we pushed and hacked our way forward beneath the overarching rainforest canopy. At times it was like taking a steam sauna with assorted monkeys, gorillas, biologists, and pygmies, and being the only primate who seemed to notice that the sauna door had locked behind us. Being in tundra so soon afterward made me feel both wonderfully fresh and uncluttered, and also a little off balance. Maybe a little too exposed. The highest thing I might find growing in this part of the Country would be a moose eating dwarf willow. At the moment nothing at all stood in the way of the wind that blew steadily out of the northeast, hauling cold sheets of drizzle overland toward Trepassey. Nothing except my back. While water dripped off my pack, the binoculars dangling against my chest on the leeward side were perfectly dry. I picked them up and focused upon what I thought were distant caribou. They were gulls standing in a marsh. Between the mist and the complete lack of landmarks for scale I hadn't been able to tell the difference.

A mile or two later I still hadn't found any caribou. So I left the stream, whose gradual passage south had been my guide, and turned east to see what lay over the low ridge in that direction. I was careful about picking out a rock or a prominent hummock each time I moved farther ahead. In fact, I was scrupulous about it. I still had that sensation of waking up in a strange place. Being a bit disoriented to start with, I wanted to make doubly sure that I wouldn't lose my general sense of direction. General was good enough, though. There were breaks in the fog that revealed the lay of the land here and there. The road was only a few miles one way, and the coast wasn't too many miles away in the other direction.

For inspiration I had memories of the Porcupine caribou herd, which I once followed along Alaska's North Slope in the Arctic National Wildlife Refuge. More than one hundred thousand strong, streaming across the barrens like the plasm of a single

NORTHERN GANNET, CAPE ST. MARY'S,
NEWFOUNDLAND, JULY 1989

great cell, they come from taiga wintering grounds far south in the Yukon to give birth in June, and soon afterward begin the return journey. For some this circuit adds up to more than fifteen hundred miles, and, as far as I know, they navigate it every year without getting lost.

As I topped the ridge in Avalon between 350 and 400 spectral caribou appeared below. The animals were scattered near and far, less sociable than usual. The females with new suckling calves were ignoring their young of the previous birth season, forcing them out on their own. I watched several of these newly independent yearlings band together and trot on a confused-looking circuit through the herd while the older animals grazed and rested. To get a better view I passed over some smaller ridges and sat in the shelter of an isolated boulder with my arms braced against my knees to hold the binoculars steady.

When I was around caribou on the North Slope day after day, I began to call them "boo," as my companions did. What's that wolverine dragging around? Boo leg, looks like. See the plover nest in the gravel with the eggs all smashed? Must have got boo'd when the big herd came by. When we took a break from hiking, I remember, we usually found water within easy reach, collected in a depression left in the tundra by a boo hoof. We would boil it over a backpacking stove with tufts of boo moss, crowberries, a bit of lapland rosebay, whatever anyone liked: boo track tea. Drink until rested.

I realize that when boo let me get close or, better yet, walk curiously over toward me, it doesn't mean that they want my company. But it lets me enjoy the illusion that they do. Part of my attraction to these animals circles around to the fact that they used to live where I do in Montana. I feel that I'm gaining something back when I'm near them. I like the way they glide over the ground in a high-stepping trot, and I like how the spindle-legged young ones can do it within a few hours of birth. I like how the dark skin around boo eyes makes the orbs appear larger. On Avalon dark-ringed eyes gave the animals that I watched gliding through veils of mist an even more haunted quality. Too soon the time came to turn back to the road.

The fog had lifted a bit, and I took a bearing on a distant rise ahead. On the way a sandpiper took off from a pool. I followed its flight through my binoculars, trying to identify it. No luck. I followed it a bit farther. My old binoculars having expired in the Congo, I was using a brandnew pair, and I spent some more time swinging them back and forth from one object to another, getting used to the optics. Then the fog started closing in and I looked out from my turnings, and understood at once that I no longer knew which direction I had come from. Or which way to go.

I took a guess based on the wind's direction and kept on for quite a long time. I should have struck the road. Instead I found myself on a plain that looked exactly the same in every direction. I remembered my compass. I remembered that it was back in the car.

I suppose the one thing I could have counted on at that point was that the fog would grow thicker. It got so thick that I could no longer pick out features thirty feet

RED FOX WITH RABBIT, ASSATEAGUE NATIONAL WILDLIFE REFUGE, VIRGINIA, MAY 1989

ATLANTIC PUFFIN, MACHIAS SEAL ISLAND,
MAINE, JULY 1989

away clearly. Whenever I turned windward, my face collected mist so fast that beads dripped off my chin as from a faucet. I decided that I should choose a rough bearing and try to keep to it until I came to water. The streams that I remembered from a glance at the map—also back in the car—all flowed more or less north to south; that is, from the direction of the road toward the coast. The water would set me straight.

The first water I came to wasn't flowing anywhere. It was seeping around on the level, first one way, then the other. Like me. The next water was moving at a trickle, but I suddenly didn't trust it. Such a side-stream could be going any direction. I would have to follow it until it joined others and ran more directly to the coast. But that would take me farther from the road, which was . . . somewhere. I was really lost.

Incredible how completely that realization drains your warmth and energy. The residual sense of well-being that we take for granted evaporates, leaving a hollowed-out place. *Lost* is synonymous with *hopeless*. Wrecked. All at once I lacked bearings enough to even begin a real thought, and for a while could only sit in the wind and try to curse.

Eventually, I began to sort out some realities. The weather was chilly but not freezing. I had no food but enough warm clothes and raingear in my pack to get through the night. If the drizzle turned to hard rain and the wind rose to gale force, I could run in place during the night to fend off hypothermia. I could run for two or three nights if everything went wrong and a search party didn't come for some reason. If I wanted to risk wandering farther from the road and help, I might find a cluster of spruce and whittle the soaked branches down to dry wood and start a fire, because I did have both a knife and matches. What else to think about? What are the things that can go wrong? When you've been miserable enough in enough wild places for one reason or another and you trust yourself to endure any discomfort, then the only question that matters is whether or not something is going to kill you. I didn't think I was in any real trouble. I just felt seriously stupid, which is part of feeling lost.

For that matter I could be within a few hundred yards of the road. I shouted hello into the wind. The wind threw it back in my face. I shouted again anyway, not only in the hope of being heard but also to reassure myself that I was real and could do something in this ghost world. Nothing. Nothing again and again. I stood up and yelled all the curses I had mumbled to myself earlier. To my amazement figures walked out of the mist. I started to raise my hand and speak, then paused. They had horns covered with velvet.

I spoke anyway, mostly silently: Hello, boo. I'm glad you came over. I could use some company right now. Where are you coming from? Where bound? Do those darkling eyes cut through the fog better than mine? What do you smell with your heads held high like that? Human? Yes, human. But I'm only here slopping around in wet boots, going nowhere fast. I'm no threat to anyone. Ah, boo, I wish we really could talk it all over. You could tell me things about life, and I'd take them to heart. Or, well, I'd be happy if you could just toss your head in the direction of the road. You know the way, don't you? You always know your way. You could lead me there.

Atlantic puffins (Fratercula arctica) nest in large colonies on the grassy slopes of seaside cliffs, digging burrows three to eight feet deep into the soil. An enlarged chamber at the tunnel's end is lined with grass and moss, ready to receive the single egg. After hatching, the chick is fed squid, shrimp, and, above all, fish, such as the capelin this puffin is carrying back to the nest. To deliver its load the puffin must sometimes run a gauntlet of gulls and skuas that will try to pirate the fish away. Great black-backed gulls will not hestitate to take both the fish and the puffin itself. When a puffin sets forth from the colony to find food, it flies in a slow, wingtip-fluttering fashion called "mothing," which is an invitation to others to go fishing. In survival terms the bird is seeking safety in numbers. Substantial puffin colonies still exist on the coasts of Greenland, Labrador, and Newfoundland. And Newfoundland birds have been successfully transplanted to Maine, where the species was extirpated in the days of unregulated hunting and "egging"—raiding the colonies for eggs. But new trouble looms in the form of intensive inshore fishing. The boats do more than cause the death of diving puffins in nets. Having decimated stocks of larger fish, these fleets are increasingly turning to smaller species such as capelin, competing directly with the puffins for vital food around colonies. Atlantic puffins winter out on the open sea; no one is yet sure where.

181

More than half the nest of the black-legged kittiwake (Rissa tridactyla) may overhang the sea-edge ledge that this species typically chooses for rearing its young. However, the nest is built of seaweed, moss, and clods of dirt firmly cemented onto the stone with mud. Two speckled eggs are normally deposited in this grass-lined bowl. The first egg produced is generally larger than the second. The occupant of that larger egg will be born first, demand the greater share of food, and continue growing at a faster pace than its sibling, and, in many cases, finally shove the second nestling out over the cliff edge to its death. Abundant along both coasts of the continent—and locally common at a number of inland lakes—black-legged kittiwakes feed mainly on fish while floating on the water's surface. They eat molluscs and crustaceans as well, and they will steal food from other birds such as tufted puffins and from juveniles of their own species. Like many gulls, these opportunists also scavenge the leavings of humans at fishing ports and garbage dumps. And all the while they fly with the kind of pure grace and precision that makes us realize the futility of applying human moral standards to other beings.

Or at least take me with you to wherever you're going. . . . You look like spirits, standing there watching me so intently. Are you? Even a little bit? Isn't this the sort of time when the boundaries between facts and the old myths dissolve and you reveal your magic? Say something!

And the caribou took a few steps closer and said to my imagination: We live here, and it is magic enough.

Then the animals, warm, strong, complete unto themselves, lifted their heads again, keening the wind. They left. Restless now, I decided to do the same. I held my arm out like a vane directly into the wind, cocked my body at an angle to that, and marched directly ahead. Unless the wind was shifting, I had to be working my way north. Maybe I would happen onto other caribou and could bore them with crazy talk for a while.

I didn't find any more caribou. I did find a decent-size waterway. A while later I walked up from the water and onto the road. I had no idea where I was on the road, but, all things considered, that was a miniscule problem. I marched along it until headlights showed through the gray clouds. Art leaned out the window and shook his head.

"I got pretty well turned around," I shrugged.

"I've been driving back and forth honking the horn. Did you hear it?"

"The wind was going the right way, but it was so strong all I heard was the hissing."

"What did you do?" he asked.

"Talked to some caribou."

"Writers." He shook his head again. "You go out for a walk and are dumb enough to get lost for a couple of hours, and now you're probably going to make a whole story out of it."

The first Paleo-Indians to reach Labrador were probably following migratory caribou herds across northern Canada. They didn't arrive until 5000 B.C. Another two thousand years apparently went by before any of these folk reached Newfoundland. Clearly the peopling of Canada's maritime provinces began relatively late in the continent's history. But then this region was a long way from Beringia, and in no great hurry to warm up. Until four thousand years ago Labrador still had an ice cap, as Greenland does today.

The Paleo-Indians had barely settled in when they were displaced from much of eastern Canada by Paleo-Eskimos, who had been following marine wildlife along the shores from Alaska. The Paleo-Eskimos were in turn succeeded by immigrants from the Dorset Eskimo culture, then by the whale-hunting Inuit, or Thule, Eskimos.

Two technological breakthroughs contributed to the Eskimos' rapid spread across the cold fringe of the New World. The first was the kayak, fashioned from skin stretched across ribs. I can think of more perfect blends of tapered grace and practicality than a kayak, but they are all alive. I owe the inventors of this craft thanks beyond saying for skimming me with water striders through shallow swamps and

BLACK-LEGGED KITTIWAKE, CAPE ST. MARY'S, NEWFOUNDLAND, JULY 1989

Cat of the north country, the lynx (Felis lynx) pads easily through deep snow by spreading the toes of its feet. Those feet are already quite large and heavily furred between the toes—a match for the lynx's chief prey, the snowshoe hare. Like the hare, this cat is largely nocturnal, and its big, golden eyes are designed for capturing faint light. Ear tufts and a conspicuous "beard" help distinguish this fifteen- to forty-pound, three-foot-long felid from its smaller, southern relative, the bobcat (Felis rufus).
In recent decades as the importation of pelts from increasingly rare African and Asian cats was curtailed, the value of both lynx and bobcat pelts skyrocketed. The plush fur of the lynx was especially sought after, and the price for a single pelt rose to eight hundred dollars or even more. Intensive trapping pressure led to declines in both species, and game managers now face the challenge of controlling the harvest strictly enough to restore the natural abundance of these native cats.

brushy side channels, eddying me with harlequin ducks behind boulders in white-twisted rivers, and carving me trails alongside dolphins through the open sea. The second hi-tech advance was the dogsled, pulled by malemute or husky breeds, which the Eskimos built out of wolves.

The next arrivals came from the opposite direction in the form of Norsemen. They sailed from the Ice Land to the Green Land and then to the New Found Land, with Leif the Lucky continuing on around A.D. 1000 to the Vinland, as he called America. After the Vikings had come and gone Indians reclaimed portions of the maritime provinces from the Eskimos. Yet only a few generations passed before more colonists began arriving from across the Atlantic, and these white people came to stay.

As with the Indians and Eskimos, much of the European immigration to this part of the New World had to do with the whereabouts of favored prey. Basque whalers may have been sailing off Newfoundland as early as the fifteenth century. The British began establishing outposts during the sixteenth century. As far as they were concerned the real frontier to be won lay not inland but 140 miles southeast of Avalon. There the Labrador current with its wealth of nutrients and plankton washes across the shallow continental shelf, creating the spectacular fish pastures known as the Grand Banks. For a long time Newfoundland was valued primarily as a convenient depot where English, French, Spanish, and Portuguese vessels harvesting the Banks could rest and resupply.

The surest way to tell when you're over the Banks, old hands told the newcomers, is when you start seeing rafts of birds. Millions of them. You could find the place in a blinding fog by their noise. The biggest fish-eater among them is even listed as a navigation marker on the official charts. Aye, there's no mistaking that one; the creature's so heavy, it can't even fly. In summertime it gathers to breed on a little slab of rock standing off Newfoundland. Funk Island is the name. Should your crew be wanting to lay in some fresh red meat, why, you can just stop by and herd these silly bloody birds right into your boat. Last time we were there we set up cauldrons in the middle of their rookery, cooked all we could eat, salted down several hundred to store in the hold, and boiled down a few hundred more for the oil. And then, by God, we used their oil as fuel to cook and boil down hundreds more the next day.

Judging from bones and gizzard stones at archeological sites, this bird had been a valued food source for immigrants since the Paleo-Indians. By the 1840s the Europeans had used up every last one. The great auk—largest of the auk, or alcid, family and the only flightless member—was extinct. There are twenty-two other species in the family. Those still fishing off Newfoundland's shores include razorbills, the great auk's closest relative and now the largest auk; common murres and thick-billed murres; black guillemots; Atlantic puffins; and one of the smallest of auks, the dovekie.

Found only in the northern hemisphere, auks occupy much the same niche that penguins do in the southern hemisphere. Although the two families are not closely related at all, the demands of chasing fish through cold waters have produced re-

LYNX, ALASKA, NOVEMBER 1984

YOUNG SNOWY OWLS, ALASKA, AUGUST 1988

markably similar designs. Both families have plump, heat-retaining bodies with feet set far back toward the stern to reduce drag in the water. On land this gives them the sort of upright posture and awkward rolling gait that so charms and amuses our own upright species.

The name penguin was originally bestowed by mariners upon the great auk and later transferred to true penguins. It probably derives from pin-winged. True penguins can no more become airborne than the great auk could. They fly through the water instead on wings modified into flippers. Among surviving auks, the short, thick, strongly tapered wings represent more of a compromise between airfoils and hydrofoils. These birds can fly, but you might say that they paddle like mad, rather than soar, through the sky.

Special bones called uncinate processes branch from each rib to overlap the next, reinforcing the skeletal cage around an auk's heart and lungs so that these organs can keep pumping at depths where the water pressure is intense. Murres have been caught in nets set nearly six hundred feet below the surface. Which leads to another surprising fact: more adult murres now die by becoming entangled in fishing nets than from any natural cause. In a single set of nets hauled up by a Newfoundland boat a scientist counted fifteen hundred birds. Off Labrador, salmon fishermen actually catch more murres than fish some years.

In colonial times virtually all the auks suffered precipitous declines from uncontrolled hunting and "egging," or raiding of the rookeries for eggs. Fishing crews and settlers hit the murres on land and sea. The well-developed breast muscles of this diver made fine eating. Plenty of oil could be rendered from the insulating fat layers and the large uropygial gland of the tail, used by the bird to waterproof its feathers through preening. The feathers themselves made good stuffing for pillows and quilts. In addition murres were often slaughtered simply for bait. Adequate protection didn't come until nearly halfway through this century, but once better regulations were enacted, murre populations began recovering nicely. Today, with the toll from fishing nets—and oil pollution—added to mortality from legal hunting, common murres are once again on a downward curve. Thick-billed murres have already undergone serious population drops in the Canadian Arctic because of nets. Razorbill losses run high as well. Puffins have dwindled as fishing fleets turn to smaller fish, competing directly for food with these smaller auks. And the bones of the last great auks are still moldering away on Funk Island.

I will never know these Atlantic shores at full strength, then, never see all that they were capable of producing in the way of birds that fly underwater with hearts beating in bone boxes. But I know some places where the imagining is easy. To begin with, you hire a boat and head out through Avalon's Witless Bay to the three protected seabird rookeries called Gull, Green, and Great islands. They are a vision of what greeted those first wooden ships full of iron-handed men.

The closer I got to Gull Island, the more auks bubbled up from where they had been winging through the sea and skittered off to either side, making way for our

Between three and four eggs are laid in the nest of the snowy owl (Nyctea scandiaca). The interval between the laying of each egg is so long that by the time the last egg has hatched, the firstborn owlet is preparing to fly. Thus the brief arctic summer finds the female owl sitting almost continuously on her brood while the male brings her food. When not hunting, he stands off at a distance, scouting for danger. When he is alarmed, his hooting call will alert the female and send her out away from the nest to perform a distraction display. If that fails, the parents are likely to attack all but the largest predators and try to drive them away. Eider ducks and various geese will place their nests near that of an arctic owl pair to gain protection from arctic foxes. The number of eggs produced and the survival of young closely reflect the cyclical abundance of rodents in this owl's arctic environment. Pairs may not breed at all in years when their main prey, brown and collared lemmings, are at the low point of their cycle. After all, the whole courtship process for this owl usually begins with the male dancing stiffly in front of the female with his wings outstretched and a dead lemming in his beak. As many birdwatchers know, a scarcity of lemmings in the north country means an invasion of snowy owls into the Lower 48 during winter. Some have reached as far as California and Bermuda. In good lemming years these big white birds are rarely seen south of Canada.

187

MOOSE, ALASKA, NOVEMBER 1989

craft. The day was warm and foggy—capelin weather, the captain said, blowing in from the south-southeast. The Gulf Stream lies in that direction, not far beyond the Grand Banks. That's where the warm air comes from. On its way across the chilly Labrador current the moisture in the air begins to condense into fog. The reason it's called capelin weather is that the fish of that name come from the same direction, leaving their home on the Grand Banks to spawn on the beaches and inshore shoals of Newfoundland.

Later I would find their bodies washed up in glittering rows at the high tide line along with seaweed and other flotsam, for after the capelin have finished spawning, they die. Yet the eggs will hatch, and the young will migrate to the Banks, swimming with the flow of plankton. At the age of three or four they will mature and return to the same beaches to spawn. And thus each year capelin no thicker than a finger and every one doomed fill the bay to bursting with life. Not only with their own quicksilver dartings, but with the turns and plunges of herring, haddock, flounder, salmon, cod, seals, dolphins, whales, and the host of seabirds among and above them.

Gull Island is roughly a mile long and half a mile wide. Where the waves break, the rocks are draped with the brown algae called *Fucus*, or rockweed, and clustered with blue mussels. Above that is a white layer of barnacles, then a black band of the marine lichen *Verrucaria*. Then the layers of birds begin.

Black-legged kittiwakes cement their nests to the narrowest, steepest ledges with guano and mud; the islands have at least forty thousand nesting pairs. Common murres claim the broader ledges, each female laying a single egg directly onto the stone. The shell is light blue to green with touches of pink, and it is shaped more like a cone than an oval, designed to roll back and forth in a small arc if disturbed, rather than off toward the rocks below. Some authorities think that the murres may add a dab of guano to help stick the egg to the stone. I don't know how else some of the delicate ovals that I saw arrayed on slanted palisades could have stayed put. Whatever they do, it works; between seventy-five and eighty thousand pairs of murres breed on the islands.

Although thick-billed murres and razorbills both breed primarily farther north and fish off Newfoundland in the winter, a few lay eggs on the Witless Bay ledges. The eggs of a small number of black guillemots rest there as well, tucked into crevices and under the edge of boulders.

On top of the cliffs are the hummocky slopes of brome grass where puffins take over. Their eggs are hidden inside tunnels that the birds dig two to eight feet into the hillside and line with grass, peat, and seaweed. The three islands are pocked with the burrows of some 225,000 puffin pairs. They are also the perching spot for hundreds of three-year-olds that will not mate until the next year. Altogether, about two-thirds of the puffin population in the western Atlantic was crowded around us in Witless Bay. Maine not only has caribou from Avalon, it has puffins taken from Great Island between 1973 and 1981 and released on Eastern Egg Island in Muscongus Bay, where the birds had been hunted and egged out of existence by 1887. Transplanted

Largest of the deer, or cervid, family, moose (Alces alces) weigh up to eighteen hundred pounds in the case of mature males. The antlers alone may add up to seventy pounds. Long legs and powerful muscles enable adults to cope with both deep snow and the attacks of predators. Fully grown animals are all but immune to most carnivores. Examination of wolf remains reveals fractured skulls, ribs, and other broken bones that speak highly of the moose's defensive abilities. Females are notoriously aggressive in protecting their young, usually born singly and less often as twins, which remain with her for one year. Many hikers and horseback riders have tales to tell of being chased by mother moose. One female with a young calf was seen driving off an intruding grizzly. Bulls become so bellicose during the autumn rutting season that they have been recorded attacking automobiles and even freight trains that pass through their chosen mating territory.

189

as chicks and placed in artificial burrows, the puffins accepted the Maine island as their home and have been returning to breed there as adults ever since.

Like other auks, puffins must work fairly hard to become airborne and prefer a steep slope from which they can launch themselves into the wind. Having a burrow entrance that they can fly directly into and away from without walking also reduces the chance that they and their young will fall prey to their chief enemies: herring gulls and great black-backed gulls, whose nests are scattered right among the grass tussocks and farther up toward the crown of the islands. Light-boned, long-winged, able to step straight up from the ground and onto a breeze, the gulls can use gentle and steep slopes alike.

When it attacks a puffin, a gull isn't always intent upon killing the auk. It will settle for the capelin or other fish that the puffin is carrying in its bill to feed young in the burrow. Science does not call it stealing, wishing to avoid the moral overtones of that word. Fair enough. Unfortunately the term used instead—kleptoparasitism—tends to make simple fish-robbery sound like the work of a disease organism in need of psychological counseling. The real kleptoparasites among birds are skuas and jaegers, strong, agile flyers that make much of their living pirating food on the high seas and around rookeries. They may force a puffin to drop its load of fish or take the fish from a gull that has just kleptoparasitized a puffin. Or the great skua may snatch away the puffin that a gull has killed.

So far we have something like three-quarters of a million individual birds stacked up on the islands, and we haven't really looked closely yet at the top, with its mixture of meadows and wind-stunted spruce and balsam fir. There, waiting in holes for the night to come so they can fly off to feed without being snatched out of the air by the gulls, are three-quarters of a million *pairs* of Leach's storm petrels. Witless Bay is the world's second largest breeding colony of these wide-ranging birds, which touch land only to nest and spend the rest of their lives at sea. A biologist took one pair from here to Australia and released them, the captain told me as we rounded a point of Gull Island. The petrels were back at the same hole two weeks later. They weighed a bit more than they had when the biologist first captured them.

Now the total becomes 2¼ million birds here, processing fish and sometimes each other, re-creating their kind. Even with the petrels tucked away in their holes, each island zoopolis seemed packed wing to wing, and the surrounding air was fogged with birds in flight. Their combined voices surged back and forth across the rocks like surf.

Among the sounds I heard voiced by the puffins was a growl. They utter it when they fight over territory, locking their big parrotlike bills together, flailing each other with their wings, and twisting their necks to throw the other off balance. Typically they become so engrossed in battle that you could walk over and practically pick them up before they paid you any attention. Now and again, they tumble together down the grassy hillside, still locked and growling. And if neither is willing to ease its grip, or if one has hooked a sharp toe in the other and can't shake it free, they may

THICK-BILLED MURRES AND BLACK-LEGGED KITTIWAKES, CAPE ST. MARY'S, NEWFOUNDLAND, JULY 1989

POLAR BEARS, MANITOBA, NOVEMBER 1983

spill on down the rocks and into the sea. Two combatants toppled off a cliff to land in front of our boat. And as we passed by they were beginning to circle one another while swimming, still shaken but preparing themselves for another round.

Prime burrow sites with the right degree of steepness and good soil for digging are usually in limited supply. Those are the ones most fought over early in the season as the birds establish territories, and those are the ones with the best survival rates of young. Obviously they are worth tumbling down a cliff for. But just as obviously, if you watch for a while, puffins can discuss other options first in body language.

A territory owner asserts his rights by what observers call the pelican walk. The bird stands erect while raising and lowering each foot in turn, slowly, stiffly treading in place. A less aggressive signal of ownership is the spot-stomp, a sort of watered down version of the pelican walk. If a puffin alights away from his or her burrow amid other territories, it keeps its wings uplifted and its body horizontal. This is an appeasement posture, the opposite of aggression, so the body is held the opposite of erect. The closer a puffin lands to others, the longer it holds the postlanding display. And it stays bent over as it proceeds back to its hole, easing along past its neighbors in what is known as the low profile walk. Oh, excuse me. Nice morning, heh-heh. Whoops! Gracious; didn't see you there. Beg pardon. Hi, just passing by.

At home the social discourse of puffins continues. The reunited pair—partners for life, as are all auks—swing their bills, nibble and nuzzle, bill and coo, bow and shake their heads, each movement conveying information and reinforcing the bond between the male and female. Lustiest-looking is the display in which the two cock their tails and strut in a circle, knocking their bills together broadside. When one wants the other to go with it into the burrow, it stands at the entrance and looks repeatedly down the hole, then back at its mate.

Another signal of intent is what is called the moth flight. As a puffin takes off from the colony it holds its wings higher above the body than usual and flies mainly by fluttering its wingtips. This cuts its airspeed in half and makes the bird more conspicuous, which is the whole idea. Mothing means that the animal plans to leave for the sea to feed and would like others to join it. Call it a puffin invitation to go fishing.

Upon returning to the nesting area puffins often perform a group flight pattern termed the wheel. It also occurs when a colony is disturbed. A number of birds begin flying the same direction in a fairly tight pattern and are joined by more and more of the others in the vicinity until a wheel of wings surrounds the breeding grounds. Most observers think that this must be an antipredator behavior, like the schooling of fish in the sea below. Gulls do appear less willing to swoop into a halo of swarming puffins than into a smaller flock, and less able to isolate a single target successfully. But the truth is that no one is certain what puffin wheels are all about. We know only that they transcend the line past which an intensely sociable group of individuals becomes a kind of supraorganism, rotating over the place where it makes more of itself.

The concept of a supraorganism wheeled through my mind again on the southwestern shore of Avalon at Cape St. Mary's, where I sat high on the headland cliffs

A mother polar bear (Ursus maritimus) greets her twin two-year-old cubs after a brief separation on a frozen lake adjacent to Hudson Bay. For much of the year these most carnivorous of North American bears drift with the ice floes across the arctic seas, hunting seals. In October or November pregnant females congregate in traditional ranges to dig dens in snowbanks, where they will give birth. As many as two hundred females may be found in one of these maternity areas. They emerge with their cubs, usually born in pairs, sometime in March. As the weather continues to warm through the summer many polar bears come ashore to forage on plants, the abundant nesting birds found along the arctic coastline, and the occasional beached whale. During their second winter the cubs remain abroad with their mother on the pack ice to hunt. If an especially bad storm sets in they may excavate a temporary den for shelter, like human wanderers taking refuge in a snow cave or igloo.

193

By analyzing trace elements, especially metallic ones, in the flight feathers of a mallard (Anas platyrhynchos) researchers can pinpoint the area where that particular animal has recently spent time. The promise that this technique holds for studying annual movement patterns is obvious. But one metal shows up far too often in the tissues of mallards and waterfowl: lead. A single pellet ingested from a muddy pond bottom in the course of foraging can kill a mallard. And it is estimated that an average of fourteen hundred lead pellets from shotgun shells are left behind in a pond for every duck carried out by a hunter. Species as big as trumpeter swans have begun falling victim to direct lead poisoning. Meanwhile many birds that die of diseases do so because they were first weakened by an accumulation of lead in their bodies. Unless more hunters switch from lead shot to stainless steel pellets, clouds of waterfowl such as the mallard flock lifting off here may become a memory of days gone by.

overlooking a breeding colony of gannets. I sat there for hours in the warm sun and the cold onshore wind, trying to think of how best to describe what was before me: white birds with gold-tinted heads and wings more than five feet across; thousands upon thousands of them, illuminating a huge palisade from top to bottom and gliding across its face while the water raised up against the land, broke into white swirls, withdrew, and raised up anew, until I lost track of all my thoughts and concentrated on the wings I felt growing out from my shoulders. Everything seemed to be soaring. The cliffs. The high cloud wisps. Myself. The humpback whales chasing capelin beneath the waves. Their flukes—their whale wings—were so long that they resembled two light-colored young whales trailing alongside the dark grown animal.

At one time I had ten whales in view. Some were breaching far out toward the blue-glittering horizon. Some closer in were rolling and circling, working together to cast nets of bubbles around capelin schools. Herd the fish together, hold them in place with shining bubble curtains, then pass through their midst with whale mouth agape. Any commercial fisherman would understand this recently discovered whale strategy. My question is: Does it qualify the humpback as a tool-user? While three humpbacks steamed by within yards of the shore, gannets plunged through their spray and into the depths like stilettos, trailing a blue sheath of bubbles from the impact. Murres and kittiwakes formed flotillas nearby on the water and lined the ledges to either side of the chief gannet colony.

The colony itself is called simply Bird Rock. Yet the scene looked like some millennial vision by the nineteenth-century engraver Gustave Doré, who illustrated Dante's *The Divine Comedy.* The gannet host aloft could have been his angels, yearning toward the pure white of the sun while leviathan rolled below in the deep. At the same time I saw the gannets as what most scientists now agree birds are: the surviving line of dinosaurs. The reptilian scales may have been split into fluffy feathers, but the bright reptilian eyes remain—and met mine each time one of the creatures momentarily hovered beside me where the wind broke over the cliff top. Then the modern archoaur would slip the air from beneath its wings and slide away back into the pageant. One moment the white colony on the cliff seemed like an encrustation of something still more protean from the sea. The next moment hundreds of gannets would cascade off their perches into the air, and it seemed more like this white patch of earth was something that had ripened and was giving off windborne seeds.

Paradise. Saurian breeding grounds. Bursting seedhead. You see, I never completely gave up looking for a way to describe the view from my perch. Yet in the end I decided metaphors couldn't serve. There is nothing in heaven or on earth *like* what I was seeing. There was the incomparable offering of the thing itself: gannets and whales and smaller birds and fish and sunlight at the meeting of the land and the sea. They don't need to be anything except allowed to exist. The caribou had passed me the same message on my way to Cape St. Mary's from Trepassey. We live here. It is magic enough.

The glory is in each creature, and it is in their lives together and in our life among

MALLARDS, RIFLE NATIONAL WILDLIFE REFUGE, BRITISH COLUMBIA, DECEMBER 1989

MOTH ON PINE TREE, HOG ISLAND,
MAINE, JULY 1989

them. Some do manifest the qualities of a supraorganism. But the real supraorganism is nothing less than our world. I think that is the concept borne home at the ocean's edge.

The whales out there had come to Newfoundland from the Caribbean. Atlantic leatherback turtles had come from the tropics, too, and had already passed by on their way to feed on jellyfish in the arctic summer light. Thick-billed murres now breeding in those high latitudes would come to winter off Cape St. Mary's. And many of the young would swim the first six hundred miles of the trip, because if they lingered at the nest site until they were able to fly, winter might catch them and lock them away in ice. Meanwhile the puffins of Newfoundland would be wintering someplace out on the Gulf Stream, though no one has yet figured out where.

The gannets of Cape St. Mary's would leave for the Gulf of Mexico. And the sooty shearwaters and skuas roving over the Labrador current would return to the tip of South America to breed. The lesser golden plovers nesting in Avalon's peatlands would migrate to Argentine pampas; the white-rumped sandpipers—I would bet that's the kind I was watching when I got lost in the Country—would end up in Tierra del Fuego. The wheatears would head for Africa. The colossal basking sharks that sieve plankton close to shore would simply drop to the bottom and go dormant.

All the sharks had to do to resume their place here next spring was wake up. But the return of nearly every other creature, from pilot whales and harbor seals to phalaropes and warblers, would depend upon what conditions were like in a more distant part of the world. At the same time conditions in other parts of the world would be influenced by what was flowing out of the mouths of North America's rivers and out its factory smokestacks, and by changes in its forest cover, and by patterns of consumption of foreign products among North American citizens.

At a cafe in the town of St. Bride's near Cape St. Mary's, I met a visitor from Massachusetts. Like me, he had come to watch the whales and gannets. A lifetime birdwatcher, he had begun in his later years to suspect that he wasn't seeing as many songbirds as he used to around his home, and that it wasn't simply because his eyes were no longer as sharp. He went back through his journals and counted numbers. He was right; there weren't as many. Turning the woodlands of the American Southeast into monoculture plantations of soybeans and pine cost him his juncos and towhees. Destruction of the forests in Central America for firewood, lumber, and cattle pastures took black-throated green warblers, chestnut-sided warblers, Swainson's thrush, wood thrush, veery, and least flycatchers out of his account. This man, I thought, scanning the other diners in the cafe, knew the full price of a meal.

Everyone alive is an environmentalist. Some realize it and some don't. The interconnectedness of living things explains how we all exist in the first place. How we shall exist in the years to come will depend upon the wealth or poverty of the kingdom we inhabit. And the sea repeats it endlessly to the coast, as it has since the beginning: there is only one kingdom, and only one kingdom, and only one kingdom on earth.

In their caterpillar form a number of moth species are considered pests, since they may do considerable damage to crops. They can also seriously reduce wild foliage from sagebrush to conifers during cyclical outbreaks. But as adults many moths are invaluable pollinators, and some plant species would not exist at all without particular species of moths. Active during the night hours, moths often rely upon cryptic patterns of coloration to help avoid being eaten by birds and other predators during the day.

NORTHERN FUR SEAL, PRIBILOF ISLANDS, ALASKA, JULY 1986

Additional Photographic Notes

P16 BLACK-TAILED DEER, OLYMPIC NATIONAL PARK, WASHINGTON, AUGUST 1984

A Columbian black-tailed deer (Odocoileus hemionus columbianus), the Pacific Northwest subspecies of mule deer, watches the approach of an intruder in its mountainside meadow. The nearly mule-size ears for which the mule deer is named help alert it long before potential danger draws near. Columbian blacktails are thought to have less need to drink than other deer because they ingest so much moisture during the course of feeding in their rainy, mist-curtained coastal environment. Most herds make vertical migrations between flowerlit summer meadows high in the mountains and lower elevation wintering grounds. Sitka deer (Odocoileus hemionus sitkensis), the mule deer subspecies native to Alaska's Panhandle, also go by the name of blacktails, having the same dark fur covering the top of their tails.

P17 HOARY MARMOT, CANADIAN ROCKIES, ALBERTA, JULY 1989

The hoary marmot (Marmota caligata) is named for the frost white fur on its head and shoulders. The piercing warning whistle of this eight- to twenty-pound rodent is often heard in high-mountain meadows and talus slopes from northern Alaska to Washington, Idaho, and Montana. Hoary marmots are inquisitive creatures, and it is not unusual to see them interacting with playful or curious mountain goat kids. The animal finds refuge from its main enemy, eagles, and other predators in burrows beneath boulders. But grizzly bears sometimes roll the rocks aside and dig apart the underground tunnels to get at the marmot, especially when it is in hibernation. Hoary marmots go into their dens as early as September and enter a dormant state. Their respiration rate and heartbeat become extremely slow, and their body temperature falls to a point only a few degrees above freezing. They don't emerge until June, nine months later. Even then they may still have to tunnel upward through a lingering snowpack to reach the light. Perhaps as an adaptation to the demanding alpine environment, hoary marmots are more sociable than other marmots such as their common eastern relative, the woodchuck or groundhog. They live in colonies with comparatively little aggression between adults, and the young are not driven out when they mature. Maturity takes two years to reach, a long time by rodent standards. Such slow development reflects the extended hibernation period required to survive in this animal's high-country niche.

P40 ARCTIC FOX, ALASKA, JULY 1982

Compared to North America's other four fox species, the arctic fox (Alopex lagopus) has noticeably small, rounded ears, short legs, and a short muzzle. It is an example of Bergmann's rule, which states that the northern forms of an animal will have shorter appendages in relation to body size than more southerly forms. This reflects the need to conserve warmth in cool climates by reducing the surface area through which heat is lost. A certain percentage of arctic foxes have fur that turns from blue-gray to the silvery blue color of an iceberg with the onset of winter. For most the thick fur is brown in summer and pure white in winter. Like the equally white snowy owl of the Arctic, the arctic fox relies mainly upon lemmings for its meals, and its numbers echo the cyclical ups and downs of the lemming population. During summer arctic foxes help feed both themselves and their large litters of pups by adding to their diet some of the great numbers of birds that wing north to nest in the boggy tundra with its rich seasonal concentrations of insect life. In winter the arctic fox may follow another frost white species, the polar bear, across the pack ice, scavenging the big predator's kills of seals and walrus. Some of these little seven- to fifteen-pound members of the canid, or dog, family cover more than a thousand miles before returning to mate and den in spring.

P41 ALASKAN BROWN BEARS, BROOKS RIVER, ALASKA, JULY 1987

As brown bears (Ursus arctos) gather along streams to catch salmon running in from the sea to spawn, squabbles over prime fishing sites break out from time to time. These are usually settled through harmless threat displays, but when negotiations break down, sparring matches may occur. The Brooks River, where as many as twenty or more bears may congregate along a single short stretch of water, offers spectacular opportunities for viewing such behavior. However, not all cuffing, biting, chasing, or roaring should be interpreted as aggression. Very often it is simply how these giants play, and play is more common than serious fighting, especially among younger animals such as the two pictured here. Even a solitary, older bear will sometimes entertain itself by sliding down a snowbank, lying on its back juggling a log, or blowing bubbles beneath the water and pricking them with its five-inch-long claws as they rise to the surface.

P58 PRONGHORN, UTAH, NOVEMBER 1989

Pronghorns (Antilocapra americana) are one of the few hoofed animals that can easily digest most varieties of sagebrush. Some populations rely upon it as winter food when snow covers shorter vegetation. But the species as a whole is by no means tied to this aromatic shrub. Grasses and wildflowers form a vital part of their diet. This is particularly true during the spring growing season and also in early summer as the young, usually born as twins, begin feeding on their own. Originally abundant from southern Canada to northern Mexico, pronghorns thrived in the savannas of the Great Plains as well as in the high, shrub-dotted deserts of the interior West. Altogether they may have been as numerous as bison, numbering in the tens of millions. By 1910 just fifteen thousand or so pronghorns remained in North America. Today the population is approaching one million. These unique hoofed animals have prospered best on the shortgrass prairies east of the Rockies in Montana and Wyoming. In the more arid landscapes of the Great Basin and adjoining deserts they are limited by intense competition from livestock for scarce forage.

P59 KINGSNAKE, SIERRA NEVADA, CALIFORNIA, AUGUST 1989

The brightly banded California mountain kingsnake (Lampropeltis zonata) is sometimes called the coral kingsnake. The genus Lampropeltis, which includes kingsnakes and milk snakes, is widespread from Canada to South America, and the banded color pattern of several varieties resembles that of the smaller but venomous coral snake found in subtropical regions, including several southern states. By mimicking that lethal snake, Lampropeltis, which is nonpoisonous, presumably gained a certain measure of protection from predators at some point in its evolutionary history. Interestingly, several of the less gaudy kingsnakes hiss, rattle their tails, and strike when disturbed, mimicking the aggressive behavior of rattlesnakes. Kingsnakes and milk snakes are renowned as eaters of other snakes, killing them by constriction. They are immune to the venom of rattlesnakes, which form an important part of their diet in some locales. The particular subspecies of California mountain kingsnake pictured here, the San Diego mountain kingsnake (Lampropeltis zonata pulchra), is believed to feed more on lizards, birds, and smaller rodents than on other snakes. Occurring from sea level chaparral habitats to high-altitude conifer forests, it prefers moist sites such as streamsides and shady groves with rotting logs, and grows to a length of about three feet.

P80   ROSEATE SPOONBILLS AND WHITE IBIS, DING DARLING NATIONAL WILDLIFE REFUGE, FLORIDA, JANUARY 1989

Four roseate spoonbills (Ajaia ajaja) are joined by a single white ibis (Eudocimus albus) among the mangrove roots. The setting is the five-thousand-acre J. N. "Ding" Darling National Wildlife Refuge in Florida. Darling, a Pulitzer Prize-winning cartoonist as well as an ardent conservationist, was the founder of the National Wildlife Federation. Ibises feed by probing. Spoonbills feed somewhat like flamingos, by sweeping their bills through the water. But rather than catching small organisms by straining them through filters, flamingo-style, spoonbills wait until they feel fish, crustaceans, or aquatic insects within their mouths, then clamp their big mandibles shut on the prey. They are said to make grunting noises while foraging this way. At the water's edge they often nest in mixed colonies with egrets, herons, and, at times, ibises. Elsewhere white ibises nest in very large colonies of their own, and some of their late summer roost sites may hold up to eighty thousand of these birds at once.

P81   MUTE SWAN, BRIGANTINE NATIONAL WILDLIFE REFUGE, NEW JERSEY, MAY 1987

This is one of the swans that originally inspired so much European poetry and dance: the mute swan (Cygnus olor). Introduced to the United States from the Old World, it has prospered in the Atlantic coast states, proving to be an

aggressive competitor for territory and food. Its range has expanded to the point that mute swans are displacing native populations of the tundra, or whistling, swan (Cygnus columbianus). Mute swans are not entirely silent. They sometimes make loud grunts and snoring noises during interactions, and they often hiss when annoyed.

P100   SANDHILL CRANES, NEW MEXICO, FEBRUARY 1987

Not all populations of sandhill cranes (Grus canadensis) migrate. For example, the subspecies pratensis, the Florida sandhill crane, which is slightly smaller than typical sandhills, is sedentary. Partly because of this reliance upon a particular area year-round, it is one of several subspecies now seriously threatened by drainage of wetlands. Other sandhills, however, travel great distances from Mexico and the southern United States to nest in northern marshlands and tundra. To some extent the routes they follow may reflect patterns of recolonization after the retreat of the great Ice Age glaciers that covered most of the nothern continent. Some sandhills leave wintering grounds on this continent to breed in eastern Siberia. During winter large flocks of sandhills roost in the safety of watery areas at night along with flotillas of ducks and geese, then fly off at daybreak to feed on leftover grain in surrounding fields. They also hunt rodents, frogs, and various insects. When the air temperature drops below about twenty-nine degrees, the legs, normally outstretched in flight, are drawn in toward the body. Cranes take their name from the Anglo-Saxon word cran, meaning "to cry out." And the sound made by flocks of these four-foot-tall birds is an unparalleled concert of rattling croaks and sirenlike cries. Human tribes in North America and throughout the world developed dances that mime the spectacular courtship rituals of cranes, in which the birds leap high into the air with "craned" necks while holding out their wings spanning seven feet or more.

P101   RED FOX, MOUNT MCKINLEY NATIONAL PARK, ALASKA, MARCH 1988

The bushy tail of the red fox (Vulpes vulpes) makes up at least a third of the animal's length—about forty-two inches overall, from white tail tip to moist black nose. Like wolves, red foxes are thought to mate for life, and both parents assist in rearing the young. The kits, born after a gestation period of around fifty-one days, number between four and nine. For several days immediately after birth the male carries food to his mate in the birth den. Later both parents work to supply the growing kits with fresh food. A typical red fox home range covers one to two square miles. Individuals in more northerly areas, such as this inhabitant of Alaska's Denali National Park, may require somewhat larger ranges to meet their needs.

P120   PYGMY OWL, WASHINGTON, SEPTEMBER 1988

Active at dawn and dusk and often through the day, the northern pygmy owl (Glaucidium gnoma) breeds west of the Rockies in mixed forests of conifers and deciduous trees. While it may take insects and other birds at times, it relies mainly on rodents for food. This little bird carefully picks away the flesh from its kill and leaves the rest, rather than eating prey whole and regurgitating the bones and hair in pellets as larger owls do. Like its still smaller relative the elf owl, the northern pygmy owl is likely to choose an abandoned woodpecker hole for its nest. During courtship the male practices ritual feeding, offering the female presents of freshly killed food.

P121   PIKA, CANADIAN ROCKIES, ALBERTA, NOVEMBER 1989

An inhabitant of high-altitude talus slopes and boulder fields, the pika (Ochotona princeps) is a tailless, round-eared, chipmunk-size member of the order that includes rabbits and

hares. Fur-soled footpads give it extra traction on the rocky terrain it traverses in search of grasses and wildflowers. Because it does not hibernate, it must gather enough food during the brief mountain summer to last through the snowbound months, which add up to more than half the year at such elevations. Also known as the cony and the rock rabbit, the pika may be seen spreading mounds of its food cache on rocks near its den to dry in the sun—a trait that has given it yet another name, the haymaker. It marks these piles with both urine and scent from a facial gland, and defends them against neighboring pikas. The pika's piping call of warning is a common sound across the high country's cliffy areas. Its major enemies appear to be birds of prey and the occasional weasel. Losses are balanced by the females' ability to produce several litters of up to a half-dozen young between spring and late summer.

P132   PORCUPINE, IDAHO, JUNE 1988

The porcupine (Erethizon dorsatum) is a large rodent that waddles slowly along on short legs. But as many a young and inexperienced predator has learned, this creature is anything but an easy meal. The barbed quills—specialized hairs—that cover much of the body grow thickest along the lower back and tail. They are not really flung or "fired" at intruders as folklore would have it. Yet the porcupine can arch up and slap its tail into an enemy so quickly it sometimes seems that way. Moreover, loose quills may actually fly into the air during such a maneuver. Timber plantation managers are concerned with the porcupine's effects on young trees. It often girdles them in its quest for the cambium layer—the nutrient transport system of woody plants located just beneath the bark. Foresters might consider whether the basic problem is the porcupine or the fact that native populations of the fisher and the wolverine have been eliminated from much of their original range. These large members of the

TREE FROG, WASHINGTON, SEPTEMBER 1978

WHITE-TAILED PTARMIGAN, WASHINGTON, NOVEMBER 1987

mustelid, or weasel, family, are among the few carnivores that regularly and successfully hunt porcupines.

P133   ELK, YELLOWSTONE NATIONAL PARK, WYOMING, JANUARY 1989

A bull elk (Cervus elaphus) wades through deep snow on the Yellowstone Plateau among charred trunks of lodgepole pine. During the fall of 1988 the media spoke of a holocaust here. Fires were described as "ravaging" the countryside and "destroying" this well-loved national park. In fact, less than a quarter of Yellowstone National Park was seriously burned. And both elk and lodgepole are well adapted to fire to begin with. It could even be said that they exist here in good part because of fires, which appear to have swept through western forests at fairly frequent intervals since prehistoric times, recycling nutrients and creating openings for grazing animals. So predictable a force is fire in these ecosystems that lodgepole pines produce two kinds of cones. The first is a typical seed-bearing pine cone. The second type, called a serotinous cone, is heavily sealed over with resins and will open only in the heat of wildfire, seeding the ash-rich ground with new lodgepole.

P168   NORTHERN GANNETS, CAPE ST. MARY'S, NEWFOUNDLAND, JULY 1989

Northern gannets (Sula bassanus) nest in colonies atop sea cliffs and protected islands, choosing relatively flat areas where available. They come together in such large numbers that a handful of colonies hold nearly all the gannets of the northern Atlantic. Nonbreeding birds less than three or four years of age form subcolonies on the periphery of each main nesting area. The nests themselves are quite evenly spaced as a rule, each one being just out of reach of the neighbors' sharp bills. Breeding pairs, which stay together from one year to the next, take turns incubating the single large egg. A gannet that is ready to take a break from brooding will

stretch its long neck skyward and flex its wings to show its intentions as its mate flies by. Upon each exchange of duties the pair performs an elaborate bowing, bill-dipping, and mutual preening ceremony. The young hatch out after forty-two to forty-four days, and are fed regurgitated fish. As the young grow older, the parents bring whole fish in their beaks. Another three months pass between hatching and the time the big juveniles are ready to leave the nest. Their first flight may consist of little more than a long glide down off the cliff into the ocean.

P169   HARBOR SEAL, MONTEREY PENINSULA, CALIFORNIA, SEPTEMBER 1989

Harbor seals (Phoca vitulina) eat squid, octopus, and various mollusks and crustaceans, submerging for twenty minutes or longer at a time, and reaching depths of as much as three hundred feet. Because they also feed on fish, including species such as salmon and herring, they are often shot on sight by commercial fishermen. Canada has even placed a bounty on these competitors.

P198   NORTHERN FUR SEAL, PRIBILOF ISLANDS, ALASKA, JULY 1986

Capable of swimming at seventeen miles per hour, northern fur seals (Callorhinus ursinus) chase squid, fish, and more than two dozen other kinds of marine animals. Once decimated by both Russian and American commercial hunters for their pelts, which contain three hundred thousand sleek hairs per square inch, northern fur seal populations now contend only with a tightly controlled harvest of nonbreeding bachelor groups. Distributed from Alaska to the Baja Peninsula, these animals migrate toward traditional northern breeding grounds each spring. Many return to islands in the Bering Sea controlled by the Soviet Union. But the greatest number—nearly a million and a half—congregate on the Pribilof Islands off the coast of Alaska. Large,

dominant males, usually ten years old or older, show up first and battle to establish breeding territories. Younger, subordinate males are soon banished to bachelor beaches elsewhere. Each dominant male attempts to gather arriving females, which weigh just 130 pounds to the male's 600 pounds, into a harem of as many as forty or fifty. Any pregnant females among them will give birth first and then mate several days afterward.

P201   TREE FROG, WASHINGTON, SEPTEMBER 1978

You can find the Pacific tree frog (Hyla regilla) between the Rockies and the Pacific coast, from southern Canada to Baja, and from sea level to nearly the top of the Sierra Nevada. Members of the tree frog family, Hylidae, can be told by their small size, enlarged toe pads, and loud peeping voices during the early spring mating period. In fact, the name of the common hylid of the East is the spring peeper (Hyla crucifer). A female spring peeper less than an inch and a half long may deposit as many as a thousand eggs among the submerged vegetation, ensuring choruses for the years to come. The Pacific tree frog comes not only in green but also in gray, brown, tan, and tones of black. Some of this simply reflects genetic variation between individuals. But the same frog can change from light to dark within the space of a few minutes, altering its pigmentation to better blend into its background.

P202   WHITE-TAILED PTARMIGAN, WASHINGTON, NOVEMBER 1987

Like the snowshoe hares and ermine farther down the mountainsides, this bird of western peaks, the white-tailed ptarmigan (Lagopus leucurus), molts from brown to snowy white as winter arrives. It also grows a longer set of claws useful in burrowing through the snow in search of food, shelter during storms, or concealment and escape from enemies. The long claws

also act as snowshoes. More important in that respect, though, are the stout feathers growing between the toes. These increase the ptarmigan's load-bearing surface by 400 percent, halving the depth that its feet sink into the snow. Both the toe feathers and the set of long claws are shed in summer. Found above timberline from the Arctic to the Montana Rockies, with isolated populations as far south as New Mexico, white-tailed ptarmigan produce four to eight eggs that hatch after an incubation period of just over three weeks.

P204   SHORT-BILLED DOWITCHERS AND DUNLINS, GRAYS HARBOR, WASHINGTON, APRIL 1989

Both short-billed dowitchers (Limnodromus griseus) and dunlins (Calidris alpina) nest in northern marshes and tundra, then winter along the coastline of the southern United States and Mexico, with the dowitchers continuing as far south as Brazil. They migrate between these ranges in large mixed flocks with other sandpipers and plovers. Five sites in North America regularly support more than a million shorebirds during migrations. One of these is Grays Harbor, Washington, where the birds pictured have paused to feed and rest. The resting position, with one leg drawn up against the body and the head tucked beneath a wing, reduces the animal's surface area and therefore retards heat loss. Dowitchers typically forage by wading in shallow water and rapidly probing the mud for marine worms, molluscs, and crustaceans. Dunlins take the same sort of food, but normally prefer to forage over bare mud flats after the tide has receded. "My party shot a great number of them, on account of the fatness and juiciness of their flesh," wrote John James Audubon more than a century ago. He was speaking of the short-billed dowitchers' popularity as a delicacy in the days before game laws were drawn up, a popularity that seriously depleted populations. At present the limiting factor is coastal habitat free from serious pollution and disturbance.